THE
PLEASURES
OF THE
GAME

Other books by Colman McCarthy

In the Name of Profit
    (with Robert L. Heilbroner and others)
Disturbers of the Peace:
    Profiles in Nonadjustment
Inner Companions

THE PLEASURES OF THE GAME

COLMAN McCARTHY

The
Theory Free
Guide to Golf

THE DIAL PRESS
NEW YORK
 1977

MANUFACTURED IN THE UNITED STATES OF AMERICA
FIRST PRINTING

for Denis McCarthy,
who keeps on advancing the ball,
no matter what

Acknowledgments

I'm not going to get carried away with credits—I have a golfing date in a few minutes—but debts are owed to a few friends who helped with this book. Don Graham, George Solomon and Ken Ringle of *The Washington Post* first encouraged me to write about golf—"Don't just talk about it hour after hour!"—and their sports section of the *Post* is where some of the material here first appeared.

Going back in a straight line of affection, I have had a number of companions since my boyhood who shared their friendship where the sharing is most pleasurable, the golf course. These include my late father, John P. McCarthy, my mother Lucy McCarthy, my brothers Justin, Denis and John, and Tom Boone, Barry Montgomery, Michael McDermott, Bud Daley and Coach Bill Gardiner (all of that championship season at Spring Hill), as well as Bernard Shulman, Ed Wolfe, Sargent Shriver, Tom Deegan, Alice Russell Deegan, Jim Ryan, Jack Vardaman and Angelo Provenzano.

My editor at the *Post,* Phil Geyelin, has yet to apply his athletic skills to golf, but any day now I expect his conversion. My three boys—Jim, Johnny and Eddie—now shoot in the low 130s, and we are the happiest of foursomes, on and off the course. As for twosomes, Mav McCarthy, the woman I live with, is a beauty of mind and body, with whom I am ever playing a round.

The trouble with all of us,
who grumble over the game and thus spoil
an otherwise pleasant afternoon with congenial
friends,
is that we do not understand the game,
nor ourselves.

Bobby Jones

Contents

Preface

I turned 39 the other day, which means I've been a golfer for 31 years. My earliest efforts, as an eight-year-old, were more swipes than swings, but what seeped into my head then has never left: that the pleasures of this game are among the happiest of life's delights. That was true when I was dribbling my father's throwaway range balls that were older than I was, and it is true now when I am likely to play 45 holes some morning, afternoon and evening when work in the office becomes too much. Walter Hagen advised us to take time to smell the flowers as we pass through life. I've been doing that—except when a sun-flower or rose bush impedes my backswing—and what I'm writing here is a mix of instruction, commentary, observation and recollection to increase the chances that golf can be as pleasurable for you as it is for me. Lowering your score obviously means getting more threes and fours on your card than fives and sixes, but going lower can mean a higher awareness that golf is much more than its theories.

Golf exercises the body, stimulates the mind and elevates the spirit. It engages them in pleasurable ways that are worth all the attention we can give. My own attentions began in my boyhood when I was a member of a golfing family in one of the golfingest areas of the world: the north shore of Long Island in the Great Neck-Glen Cove-Locust Valley corridor. From our home in Old Brookville, I could bicycle to any one of a dozen nearby courses to caddy. That is what I did summers. I carried clubs mostly for what P. G. Wodehouse called "the foozlers." But some days were better than that. When PGA tournaments were held on Long Island, I found myself caddying for the legendary Tommy Bolt, or such touring pros as Billy Casper and Bob Rosburg, or such pro-am divines as the Duke of Windsor. From the caddy ranks, I moved into the pro shop as the lowest of the shop boys. But the work was enjoyable, whether making sales, cleaning clubs, picking up practice balls on the range or providing a listening service to the pro when he would expand on how he almost made it big on the tour. (One expander was big George Bayer, once the game's longest hitter.) From there, I went into darkness— working as the night waterman in charge of rotating fairway sprinklers. In between rotations, especially midnight to 3 A.M., I practiced putting by moonlight, sighting Venus in my plumb-bob on sidehill putts.

Night or day, my game was improving. I went to Spring Hill College, an Alabama school rated high in academia because its on-campus 18 hole course meant that students could read the greens as much as the books. I did more of the former, recording a 69.5 competitive scoring average in my junior year. I could go no lower, so as a senior I turned professional and helped pay my tuition by giving golf lessons to classmates who wanted to be "rounded out." In summers during college, I played at Sands Point Golf Club in Port Washington. I was club champ for two years (I should have been, what with fellow members like Averill Harriman, Rex Harrison and Perry Como offering some of the duffing competition), and was asked to give exhibitions with masters like Claude Harmon, Shelley Mayfield and Johnny Revolta.

After college and after the loafing life at Sands Point, I spent a few years atoning for those sins by living at a Trappist monastery in central Georgia. When I showed up at the gate house in yellow golf pants and alligator shirt, the lay brother in charge of work said he had just the job for me—shoveling manure. "But change out of those yellow pants first," he counseled. "You might frighten the cows." Unlike the Jesuits or ordinary clergy, less penitential and who believe that golf and salvation are compatible, the Trappists' idea of recreation goes back to the 12th century, when the Order began, and a walk through the woods (on a straight and narrow path, preferably) was sufficient sport for the soul. I played no golf for five years, as severe a penance for me as fasting was for Aquinas. After this extended layoff (and leaving before vows), I went back to the game, a born again golfer and making a leap of faith that I could recover at least the old feeling and perhaps the old touch.

For the past decade, I have been writing for *The Washington Post* as a member of the editorial page staff. Indeed, although golf is not a subject as demanding of comment as the behavior of Congress, the policies of a President or the abuses of a federal agency, it does call for an occasional editorial. In the past few years, no other editorial page in the country has been as devoted to commentary on golf: we have deplored the "no slice" golf ball invented by some Californians who called themselves scientists, applauded Jack Nicklaus when he exceeded Bobby Jones's record for winning major championships, supported the Urban Land Institute when it suggested that smaller golf courses are now in order, questioned whether amateur golfers should be restricted to archaic rules about accepting money, suggested that the Secret Service be used in other ways than as Presidential forecaddies, examined the difficulties sportswriters have in predicting winners of major championships (as hard a time as journalists have in calling the shots in political elections) and lamented the disappearance of caddies.

On occasion, demands have been made for my professional services. When Arena Stage in Washington held its annual benefit auction in June, 1975, I was asked if I would contribute a golf lesson. "Delighted," I said. I was in fine company: a script of "Our Town" autographed by Thornton Wilder, an original Oliphant cartoon and a one year membership to the Watergate Health Club were among the other offerings. But what would *I* sell for? The bidding began at $10. Instead of dropping to $5 (as my nightmare the evening before forecasted) it steadily climbed, and the audience of 900 seemed to hum when two people battled it out: $45, $50, $55, $60, $65. It topped out at $70. The winner was a fellow who had never played before and didn't know if he would ever play again. But he had a few dollars and wanted to explore. I gave him the lesson he richly craved and wished him a long and happy involvement in the game. But watch how you throw your money around, I warned.

In all of these roles—caddy, greenskeeper, amateur and professional golfer, spectator and writer—and as one who has played with the blessed (Billy Graham), the mad (Bobby Riggs), the wandering (Titanic Thompson), the skilled (Bob Goalby), the happy (my boys, Jim, Johnny and Eddie) and the endearing (my wife Mav)—the pleasures have been many. This book is offered as a call both to those who have yet to take up the game and may need a final inducement to come to their senses—and thus come to much more—and to those who are now playing but want their golfing pleasures, like their tee shots, to extend further. Yet what I hope to convey in these chapters is less distance than breadth—breadth for our ways of experiencing the game. I have written not only about some of the basic mechanics of golf—putting, the grip, bunker shots, the backswing—but also about some of the basic non-physical activities—ways of buying golf balls, selecting the number of clubs we need, picking a teaching pro, controlling temper, betting, watching tournaments, reading golf's best literature, offering commiseration, introducing children to the game and more.

All these are among the pleasures of the game. Happily, they are not the only ones, because the areas I explore will lead you to further explorations of your own. Look around, I am saying, because the pleasures of golf are within our reach, even if the mastery of the game is not. Playing well is important but less so than feeling well about the game and ourselves—elevating our spirits by getting the most out of what I, and you, know to be the most spirited and pleasurable game of all.

Colman McCarthy
Washington D.C.

THE
PLEASURES
OF THE
GAME

Left Foot, Right Knee—Help

Not long ago, a friend asked if I would give him a few tips on playing "good golf." We talked a little, and I discovered that his ambitions were more modest than I had thought. He wanted only to hit an occasionally straight shot, score a par every few holes and walk off the course with a body and spirit more at ease than when he walked on. In other words, he liked golf but he wanted to like it more.

"Read some golf books," I suggested. "It's a mental game." I named a few authors.

Some weeks passed and I saw my friend again. He had read the books all right, but he confessed that now he had less interest in playing golf. The books had killed his enthusiasm, a dousing of ice water on what had been warm ardor for the expected pleasures of the game. He allowed that he had always known that golf was a mental game, but the books he read had presented it as a complex cerebral exercise. No thanks.

When I went to read the books by which this ex-golfer had been driven off course, I had an irrational second or two when I, too, wanted to give up the game. Here was one pro telling you to "start the swing with your left shoulder. At the moment of takeaway, the very beginning of the backswing, start your left shoulder turning around your spine." Another master advised that the start of the swing "is definitely a right-handed, right-sided movement that requires a balance on the right foot." That sounded like ballet. A third came on with the theory of "the overshift." He explained that an improper backswing occurs when "the golfer tends to lift the left heel much too high, which throws the weight to the outside of the right foot and forces both body and head to move off the ball." Go for some relief to the golf magazines and their instructions offer much the same. "In a good address position," one pro writes, "the player addresses the ball opposite the left heel. This is fine, because you will be on your left foot at impact so that this ball position is a correct one. However, because the right hand is lower than the left on the club it is natural for the player to bend the right knee slightly; this bend on the right knee does balance the player on his left foot."

Left foot, right knee, left heel too high, overshift, shoulder turn: who can make sense of all that? In this tournament of theories, it is the golfer who plays for pleasure who loses. It is as though golf has been developed into an exact science, and consequently we are now advised to hit the ball by applying an algebraic formula to a geometric stance with an IBM calculator. But golf for pleasure is not like that. It is a game, which means first that felicity is essential to it. If you aren't getting pleasurable sensations from the four or five hours of an 18 hole round, you ought to drop the sport.

Actually, it doesn't take much to make a golfer happy. In fact, a small pleasure in golf can produce an elation recalled for years. As P. G. Wodehouse, the master of golf humor, wrote, "I have sometimes wondered if we of the canaille don't get more pleasure out of it than the top-notchers. For an untouchable like myself two perfect drives in a round would wipe out all memory of sliced approach shots and foozled putts, whereas if Jack Nicklaus does a sixty-four he goes home and thinks morosely that had he not missed that eagle on the seventh he would have had a sixty-three."

Most instruction books are troublesome because the heavy confusions they drum into us serve only to build up the pressure to play well. I have always thought that life's agonies were already so liberally distributed in everything else we do that there was little need for bringing them out to the golf course. Thus my goal is to offer to golfers some simple good advice, rich in experience but free of complex theories.

Often, I have discovered, the pleasures of a round of golf are created by concerns that the great teachers of the game never seem to get around to teaching—such small matters as the ability to find a lost ball when "it landed right there in the open," plotting effective strategy on the par fives, dubbing chips from off the frog hair, controlling your temper, empathizing with a playing partner who takes consecutive sevens, getting out of the woods in a single shot. And since golf is a highly individualistic game (you are the only one to touch the ball, no team member can carry you), then perhaps we need not look to someone who is immeasurably beyond us as a model for our game. If Bobby Jones could say that "Jack Nicklaus plays a game with which I am unfamiliar," what of the rest of us?

What we need familiarity with is ourselves—as we think about golf, play it, talk of it and wonder how to enjoy it more. It is, in fact, essential to pay attention to ourselves:

3 ·

our physical capacities for a start, but also our emotions, golfing habits and common sense. Golf instruction has all but been taken over by those who attempt to drum quantities of useless theory into our heads. Our favorite pro stands over the ball interminably, we stand over the ball interminably. The year's top money winner takes an extra-full swing, we take an extra-full swing. Most golf books come on so hard—laying on theories, secrets and hunches that guarantee to lower our score by 10 shots, or teach us to play by the methods of masters—that the main purpose of the game is lost: that combination of pleasure, emotional uplift and competitive excitement that is special to golf.

We aren't striving to be champions, to go on the tour and make the ball dance with backspin on every shot into the green. We go the course for our own pleasure and relaxation. This book will show the weekend golfer how to play better and enjoy the game more.

· 4

The Hazard of Thinking
Too Much

The sagest piece of golfing advice I ever received was a four word tip from a member of a ninesome I was once playing in: "Miss 'em quick, kid." The dispenser of that wisdom was an aging caddy, stoop-shouldered and bow-legged, who came out to walk around with other caddies on Mondays when the serfs were allowed to commandeer the fairways. Gangsomes—eight, nine or ten of us—were common on those caddies' days of distant summers, when we would play the course repeating the flubs and gaffs we jeered the rest of the week while carrying the overweight bags of "the members."

"Miss 'em quick": in a ninesome, how could it be any other way? Surrounded by your urchiny companions, all of them aware that precious Monday time was ticking away if you stood over the ball too long, it was either hit the ball and think later or be trampled by the masses of your own ninesome while being fired at by the tensome behind you.

Most golfers today probably never heard that old bit of wisdom. Today's golfer addresses the ball, then begins a long, slow-motion countdown interspersed with waggles of the clubhead, shifting and reshifting of feet, gazing off at the flag, five, ten, a dozen times—as though the fairway or green might suddenly begin waggling itself.

Why do we have so many golfers who stand over the ball in frozen trances? One sure cause is the example of Jack Nicklaus. A descendant of Cary Middlecoff and a contemporary of Doug Sanders, he is among the most pronounced diddlers of the game. Nicklaus stands over the ball from 30 to 45 seconds before hitting it. (I have followed him around in tournaments with a stopwatch.) He checks and rechecks the target a dozen times. He stares at the ball in a final surge of intensity. Only then does he swing away. The 90- or 100-shooter sees this and thinks, "If that's how the world's greatest does it, then I might as well give it a try." But if an ideal model is what we seek, why not take the example of the nation's merriest pro, Lee Trevino. He came from the caddy yards, so he "misses 'em quick." He picks a club, gets over the ball, takes two looks at the target and lets fly. Another worthy example is Billy Casper. He takes but a moment to hit a shot. As a boy, I caddied for Billy—in 1955 when he first came on the tour. Two other rising stars first shone that year—Gene Littler and Arnold Palmer—so Casper wasn't noticed at first. But in caddying for him in one tournament, I was amazed at his pace: step up, hit it and get to the next shot.

Those golfers who stand too long over the ball perhaps believe that because golf is a mental game you must always be thinking on the course. That isn't true. At the game's most crucial moments—at impact and preparation for impact—your head ought to be free of theories. Forrest Fezler, one of the lesser-knowns on the tour, explained part of the problem last year to *The Washington Post:* "The older you get, the more mechanical your swing becomes. You start thinking about how to shift your right leg, how to hold your hands, and you make mistakes. The more you know, the worse you score." If you need to run through a list of "things to remember"—head down, front arm stiff, knees flexed and the other pointers teaching pros make good livings trying to get you to follow—use the time walking to the ball. There is plenty of it.

When you arrive at the ball, it is time for action, not reflection. Golf is a sport in which little physical movement is demanded. If you add up the time spent on swinging the club—about two seconds a shot—it is less than four minutes that you are actually "playing" golf during your 18 holes. That time is too precious to waste on thinking.

All too often, it isn't thought that is inside the fidgeting golfer's head anyway. It is worry. Is my grip right? Are my shoulders square? Is my clubface open? Samuel Coleridge believed that "fear gives sudden instincts of skill," but I suspect the poet spent little time on the fairways. In golf fear can make you lift up your left shoulder and that leads to topping, or it makes you lunge forward on the downswing, which leads to smothering. Worse, it induces you to think about all the unsightly places where you might hit your shot. The more you delay hitting the ball, the greater the chance you will not hit it well.

None of this is to suggest that one or two practice swings should not be taken. They should; they are useful for the muscles. The wise golfer also takes a practice swing *after* the shot—to get a feel for what in the just-completed swing was right or wrong.

"Miss 'em quick" means less that a skill must be acquired than a habit dropped. To shake the fidgets or diddles, try playing nine holes in which you take no more than a few seconds to get each shot off. See what happens. Odds on, you'll be hitting more good shots, and feeling more at ease with yourself and the course.

To Your Health

We (golfers) drink too much. We live too good. I don't con-
sider myself an athlete because I'm not in good shape.
Arnie Palmer's not in good shape. Bob Murphy sits on a
walking cane between shots. Julius Boros could be one hell
of a player, but he's 20 pounds overweight and he doesn't
want to fight it.

Bob Goalby
(*Sports Illustrated,* July 20, 1970)

What Bob Goalby said of his fellow tourists is harsh but it
is true—not only for the players he knows but for most
other golfers. Few indeed "want to fight it." We have taken
golf, which could be an opportunity for toning up our

physical well-being and used it as one more occasion to let ourselves go to seed or pot. Rather than capitalizing on golf as an opportunity either to regain the health that we may have squandered or to keep fit so that no squandering can occur, many try to reduce the physical aspects of their game and their life to an absolute minimum.

I assuredly cannot boast that I am anywhere near being the caliber of golfer that I could be—who is?—but I can claim that I am one of the healthiest golfers now playing. And therein is much of the pleasure I find in the game. At 6'2" my weight is 175 and my heart rate is about 38 beats per minute. (A beat of 50 is considered good. The average is likely to be in the 60 to 80 range.) A low heartbeat is ideal because the heart muscle is then so strong that it can pump blood through the body with such power that fewer beats are needed. Forty beats per minute compared with 70 means 15 million fewer beats a year—a tremendous relief for the heart. Heart attacks happen only after years of the heart itself being attacked by neglect.

At one time in my life, I had a high pulse rate—when I was not playing golf for a five year period (between ages 22 and 27) and getting little exercise. But after taking up the game again, my pulse lowered. And it has been low since. It's playing golf that's put me in better shape, and the exhilaration of being healthy adds pleasure to many activities, in addition to golf.

For me, being on the golf course—inhaling clean air, feeling the sun and the breezes, walking on the soft turf— is encouragement to keep myself physically fit. "I want to enjoy this as long as I can and as much as I can," I say to myself. I have found the pleasures of golf are greater when I don't drink on the 19th hole, smoke on the fairways or eat junk food at the halfway house. Usually, I bring my own food to the golf course: an orange or a banana and a can of fruit juice in my golf bag is all I need. I've been doing this for so long that it's now a habit. Sometimes just an orange at the end of nine holes is plenty.

Most of golf is walking, which ensures mild exercising for the heart. But the golf course can be used for even more stimulating activity—as a running track. For several years, I have been using the fairways of a course near my home as a place to run. Its 6,800 yards are about what I like: a little more than five miles a day. I have noticed that running five miles on a golf course is almost totally different from five miles around a cinder track. The latter is boring, the ground is hard and there is always some local Frank Shorter whizzing past you to make you feel like a turtle. On the fairways, the ground is softer and thus less damaging to the knees and ankles, the scenery is more pleasant, the air purer (less lead gets into the blood because car fumes are distant) and your mind is taken off the strains of running. On the course, I try to play an imaginary round of golf as I run: loping down the middle on one hole, through the rough on another, into sand traps occasionally (if I know the greenskeepers are scheduled to rake them in the morning).

The most serious precaution about running on the golf course is the same as running anywhere: start in slowly. Spend a week or two running one hole a day. Then try for two holes and gradually build up. I can run five miles a day now, but I needed several months getting to that point. Now it is no bother. In fact, it is a daily pleasure. And I can promise this: if you put the initial effort into it—firmly resolving that you are going to run every day—you will give yourself one of life's best feelings. You will be in control of your own body. You will sleep at night. Your muscles and bones will be alive and you will have respect for yourself because you are at the weight level that is right for you.

A minor precaution: if you do begin a self-care program by eating healthy foods and getting in a daily run, don't panic if your swing temporarily falls apart. Those who shed 30 or 40 pounds may suddenly see their power gone: drives weak, irons zingless. If that happens, try weight lifting. What you lost in strength by dumping your flab, you can regain in muscle power. That's a better source of strength anyway.

An alternative to weight lifting (at least in keeping the stomach firm and the heart strong) is the situp. Lee Trevino believes in it. At 5'7" and weighing from 170 to 180, Trevino has to be careful. Any more weight and he'd become pudgy. Trevino has been on the tour for 11 years, yet he remains conscientious about his physical condition: he jogs five days a week and does 100 daily situps. Why situps? "Golf is like fighting," Trevino told the UPI at the end of the 1975 season. "When you're ready to strike the ball, your stomach gets hard. In other words, your stomach helps you when you hit a shot. You tighten your stomach. Have you ever tried to hit a golf shot with your stomach relaxed? It's not going to go anyplace."

Trevino's stomach may hold up, but he has been having back problems of late. He missed about three months of tournaments in 1976 because of them. His was golf's most publicized back case, but back-related problems are said to be common among professional golfers, from Sam Snead who withdrew from the 1974 U.S. Open to Ruth Jessen who has had spinal disc surgery. It is no mystery that golfers suffer back problems. They play a contact sport (as compared with football and hockey, which are collision sports). The "contact" is in the constant pounding of the club into the ground. In college, I was plagued by what I called "my bad back." Only after leaving competitive golf, did I realize what had been happening. By being one of those serious-minded college wonderboys who didn't miss a day of not hitting out three to four hundred practice balls, week in and week out, I was damaging both my back muscles and my spinal discs. Fortunately, neither were permanently injured. When I stopped the madness of hitting so many practice balls, my back was "cured." As for my golf without such intense practice, it didn't suffer, because I began spending the time practicing around the green, where most of the game is anyway.

Little research has been done on golf-related health problems. One of the few who has gone into the field is Dr. Carl MacCartee, Jr., a Washington orthopedic surgeon (who also has a five handicap). He told *The Washington Star* that when he sent out between four and five hundred questionnaires to golfers in Kentucky and the Washington area, about one-third complained of golf-related injuries. Dr. MacCartee said that spinal disc problems were common, the disc being like a shock absorber between the vertebrae. The damage, he said is "not so much in the form of a rupture or a herniation, but more in degeneration, such as calcification or narrowing." Perhaps you, too, should spend more of your practice time on the green.

If it's agreed that the golfer's body should be kept in the best of shape, what about his mind—not the mental part of it but the mystical part? Tony Jacklin says he has had mystical feelings of perfect control about 10 times in tournaments. "When I'm in this state everything is pure, vividly clear," he told an interviewer for *Intellectual Digest* in 1974. "I'm in a cocoon of concentration . . . I'm invincible." Johnny Miller has spoken in the same way: he told Edwin Pope of *The Miami Herald* during the 1975 Doral tournament in Miami, "I've got a mental advantage out there. Not because I'm smarter. Just because I realize what the mind can do. You can get some fantastic results by programing your subconscious. I'm serious. Literally, I'm getting into a new area, at least for me, where I feel that I can make changes in my swing without really having to undergo a physical change. I tell myself what I want to do, and sort of program it subconsciously, and in about a month I've got it."

What Jacklin and Miller are talking about is something

all of us have experienced, whether we look back on it as a time "when everything went right," when we made "a career shot" or when we played as if good shotmaking were as natural as breathing. I remember shooting a 30 for nine holes in a college match on a course in Alabama. On walking to the 10th tee, I took on what I later realized was a new consciousness. I had no notion that I could possibly get anything less than a birdie. That is what happened: a long, straight drive, a five iron four feet from the flag and a putt that fell in the middle of the hole. For the 15 minutes needed to play that hole, I was suspended. The image I had of myself was so positive that all negative reality was blocked out.

I have had only a few moments of this transcendence on the course, but I have never met a golfer who couldn't tell of his own "high." Curiously, such moments come when I run on the golf course. After an hour or so, when my emotions, muscles and lungs cry out "enough," a lifting occurs in which my strides make perfect sense. It is as though I have a new mind, and new energies take over. If I were playing golf at that moment, I would be making nothing but birdies and pars. Sometimes in the middle of a golf course run, I do indeed begin to play a mental game. I come off the course feeling much the same as if I actually were playing golf.

It isn't possible to will these states of transcendence. But we can create the conditions that at least make them possible. I suggest that the first condition involves physical health—avoiding the known enemies of the body (alcohol, nicotine, junk food) and keeping the body in fine shape. I have never reached the transcendent heights of Jacklin but I don't dismiss his talk. My own moments of transcendence are unforgettable.

Fewer Clubs and More You

During his tenure in London as the American ambassador to the Court of St. James, Joseph P. Kennedy wrote this message to his daughter Eunice, back home in Hyannis Port. "I have been getting plenty of requests from Mother re your golf clubs. Where in the name of heaven did you leave them? Or, at what golf course did you use them or to whose house did you take them on weekend parties? There is no sign of them at the embassy and we are sure we took everything away from Wall Hall. So if you can give me any clue at all, I will get busy."

This letter—included in Rose Kennedy's *Time To Remember*—reminds golfers of the pleasures of using your own familiar clubs. Rose Kennedy, who has golfed into her 80s, knew what the younger Eunice was yet to discover—

that your golf clubs become extensions of your personality, no more to be lost or scrapped than your favorite old sweater.

Questions most often asked about clubs usually concern brands and costs, but you might better consider how many clubs you really need. The rules have allowed 14, since 1938 when the USGA set the limit. Previously some professionals went trooping around with as many as 30 clubs, doing no visible good to their golf game and much harm to the collarbones of their caddies.

Unless you are on the tour—or worse, think you should be—14 clubs are too many. I have been getting along for a number of years shamelessly with nine clubs: a driver, spoon (three wood), putter, sand wedge and the irons three, five, six, seven and eight. The other clubs—the two, four and nine irons, the brassie (two wood), and the pitching wedge are seldom needed. I never learned how to play the two iron anyway, so that torment—trying for a long iron shot from the fairway—is gone. For the same distance the three wood works fine if held back at impact just slightly. The need for a nine iron is rare because the eight can be choked or the wedge powered.

Using fewer clubs provides a kind of emotional exhilaration that is one of the true enjoyments of golf: the feeling that you control the clubs, not that they control you. A seven iron, for example, can be called on for shots for men anywhere from 120 to 160 yards, and for women from 90 to 120 yards. The seven iron can be punched for a short shot or swung with a wider arc and more closed face for greater distance. There's an added pleasure in playing golf more with what we can bring to it than with what the manufacturers can provide. The less reliance on technology, the more exhilaration from reliance on ourselves.

By this standard, one of the most self-reliant golfers I've ever known was Freddie McLeod. Until his death in the spring of 1976, he was the professional emeritus at Columbia Country Club, Chevy Chase, Maryland. A tiny man, a Scot, he was best known to the public as the first golfer off the tee at the Masters every year. Two years ago he told an interviewer about a conversation in the galley during one of those tournaments: "A friend was in back of the 18th green at Augusta and I heard him ask somebody if he thought these old fellows (McLeod and Jock Hutchinson, his annual partner) would make the 36 hole cut. The other fellow said, 'I'm not worried about that. I'm worried about them making the hills.' "

Aside from his sense of humor about himself and his perennial Masters' appearances, Freddie McLeod had a more substantial reason for fame. He won the 1908 U.S. Open—with seven clubs. In the Columbia pro shop I often talked to him, occasionally about his having used exactly half the number of clubs now allowed. "We got full use out our irons," he insisted. "We closed the face for some long shots and opened it for shorter distances. Golf required a little more skill in my day."

Those with whom I play think either that I'm too poor to afford a full set of clubs (my raggy $8.99 golf bag gives them this notion) or that one of my boys has buried the missing clubs in a secret hiding place. If they continue to gawk, I tell my companions about Freddie McLeod, and recall a little golf history. In 1964 a tournament was held in Scotland that allowed only seven clubs. The top scores —it was a 72 hole event open to professionals—were not much higher than those in their regular 14 club tournaments. What a delight it would be to have a 7 club tournament as a fixture on the American tour. The winner would be a true shotmaker, not merely the guy with a hot putter on the last day.

Such a tournament isn't likely. Golf club manufacturers would turn deaf on hearing the suggestion: what would happen to their sales if Lee Trevino or Sandra Palmer won a major tournament with only seven clubs?

As it is, manufacturers work feverishly to convince golfers that low scores and new clubs are related. But the ads in golf magazines suggest the industry is talking with tees in its mouth. The Walter Hagen Company says, "To help you improve your game, we've expanded the sweet spot of the stainless steel Ultradyne II irons horizontally through a unique over-the-hosel design." Karsten offers "ping putters, color-coded irons and calibrated woods." Another firm makes clubs with "the flex-flow shaft system." Spalding hypes us with "Dy-Nertial weighting in woods and irons." Faultless has "tunnel-sole woods [that] aerodynamically increase club head speed by reducing vacuum drag."

Enough. The ancient rule of advertising blear is at work here: to sell products that are essentially the same, make the language different. Cars, televisions, coffees and beers are sold that way, why not golf equipment? In the end, the alert golfer will avoid the come-ons. Instead, he will go to the pro shop and browse in the back room among the secondhand clubs, the "pre-owned" models. Unlike cars and televisions, golf clubs cannot be constructed with built-in obsolescence. A 10- or 15-year-old set of Wilson Staffs, Mac-Gregors or Spaldings will be serviceable. My own set of Wilsons, which I bought in 1966 for $50 from an assistant pro who was about to throw them away—he had just read an ad for Dy-Nertials and couldn't resist—are as capable of winning the U.S. Open as Freddie McLeod was, though I am not.

What Rose Kennedy knew so well—her book never tells us if Eunice found those old clubs—is regularly learned by the touring pros. Hubert Green uses a putter almost as old as he is. Jack Nicklaus, after playing in the 1975 Doral-Eastern Open, announced that he was giving up on his nine-year-old driver. He replaced it with a driver that was 30 years old.

Getting Off Course

How curious that of all the major sports—from archery to water polo—golf is the only one that requires the participant to seek an area apart from the field of play for practice. And still more curious, the conditions found in these specially designated areas have little to do with those of actual play: we spend an hour hitting a bucket of balls into an open field from a rubber tee, shooting them from flat lies into unobstructed spaces, and then try to negotiate 18 holes of difficult lies and various terrains.

Hitting practice balls may limber the muscles, which is fine, except that golf is more than a muscular game; and usually, the mind needs to be more limber than the flesh. Walter Hagen discovered he could avoid pre-game practice by submerging his hands and wrists in hot water immediately before the round and achieve the same physical results as the golfer who had been slapping balls off the practice tee.

The purpose of pre-game practice is to adjust players mentally to the conditions they will be facing in actual play. Basketball players get "the feel" of the rim on the court where they are about to play, baseball infielders take pre-game practice on the diamond where they will soon be running down grounders. And with a touch of imagination, a golfer can practice in a way that will overcome the irrelevance of the practice tee, while providing some of the challenges of the course.

In every round, we face at least a half-dozen shots which cause us to stare at the ball and sigh. Because we can't find practice tees containing sidehill lies, downhill lies or various ingeniously placed obstacles, the imaginative golfer will seek the other acres of this diverse planet that provide these situations. A neighborhood park or playground is a good place to begin.

A park in my neighborhood has an embankment on its southern rim that's ideal for practicing downhill shots. In the spring every year, I spend an hour or two hitting one or two hundred balls on this bank. The mechanics are not hard: an open stance (front foot drawn back a bit), knees bent more than usual, ball off the back foot and the grip choked an inch or two. During a typical summer, I will have to handle anywhere from six to several dozen downhill lies, none of them an insolvable mystery because of my parkland practice session.

Tax money that goes into keeping that embankment in downhill condition also provides a baseball diamond. The children think the baseball area is for them, but I know the mayor of my town allots money for the diamond so that golfers can practice hardpan shots. On the golf course, hardpan is the bare spot of earth (often near a green where cart paths have been created) that leads to skilled wedge or nine iron shots over the green. On the ballfield, the basepaths have become so hardened by mid-June that nothing builds hardpan confidence more quickly than an hour of hitting iron shots from first to second base. Some diamonds ought to be left alone, because they are kept up strictly for league games; but others can be found that are sandlots for pickup games, where no one will mind an occasional stray golfer at hours when the diamond is deserted. No "secret" knowledge is essential for mastery of the hardpan shot. Its difficulty is its unfamiliarity, and the fact that few shots in golf demand more delicacy. The stance, grip and swing are about the same as for a similar shot from the grass. The difference is that the shot is either perfect or flubbed, with little in between. The balance can be shifted toward perfect shots by a session a season on the playground hardpan.

From the playground the imaginative golfer can be lured to the trees. Get behind an oak or birch and hit out a few dozen balls from under the branches. Forget about a target. Concentrate only on firm but low shots with a four or five iron. Most players, without such practice, tighten up with frustration and impatience when behind trees, as though expecting the world to pass them by while they watch sidelined in the woods. Consequently, shots are commonly smothered and skitter only a few yards. If it appears easier to take your club and hit over the limbs of the oaks and birches rather than under, that's because the space above the tree—the whole sky—looks wider. But practicing shots under the branches will prepare you for situations you're sure to face in every round, however improbable you have convinced yourself that will be.

After you've practiced in the parks and playgrounds in the early dawn or late evening when the dog owners won't be bothering you with their unleashed animals, take a trip to the shore and practice bunker shots on the sand. I have been doing this for years on Fire Island. Although the areas toward the western end of the island are populated, the crowds disappear as you walk east past Point O'Woods and the Sunken Forest. The sand is fine and flaky there, and ideal for practicing bunker shots. Because Fire Island has no golf courses, coming over on the ferry with your clubs means you'll probably attract a few stares. Explain yourself to the curious: "I'm practicing my trap shots." New Yorkers have a high toleration for eccentricity and love direct answers.

Whenever with time to spare you spot a pond, think of your golf game: that isn't merely a pond, it's a water hazard. Park the car, give the kids in the back seat a copy of Heidegger's metaphysics and head for pasture and pond. After clearing a hundred or so shots over the soup, you'll stride back to the car ready for anything, even the kids' questions about Heidegger. Check first with the owner of the land before hitting your shots. Incidents have occurred.

For a change of pace, place a portable radio a few feet from your practice spot. Turn on the top Top Forty or the all-news station, and then begin hitting away. Concentration will be all but impossible at first, but slowly you'll learn to turn off the noise. With golf course silence becoming rare, and so many courses being built around housing developments or next to highways, the ability to tune out is becoming more valuable. Pros playing the Inverrary course in south Florida at the Tournament Players Championship in March, 1976, complained that the spectators' talking bothered them; and, believe it or not, the spectators in this instance were talking from the balconies and living rooms of their homes overlooking the fairways.

If the best you can discover for off course practice remains the flat acres that course managements provide, one alternative still persists: create variety amid the flatness. I remember shagging balls for Billy Casper in a PGA tournament in 1955 when Billy had first come on the tour.

Rather than simply smack Wilson Staffs straight out at me, he would hit five shots to my left, then five to my right, another five to the left and another five to the right. "It keeps my head working," he explained. I said to myself, this guy is going places. Neither of us knew it 22 years ago, but Billy was right about practicing and I was right about him.

Get a Grip on Yourself

After he won the Pensacola Open in the spring of 1975, Lee
Elder was invited to play with President Ford. They got
together one afternoon at the Congressional Country Club
outside of Washington. Following the round, Elder re-
vealed that the trouble with Ford's game was that "his left
hand was turned too far toward his right shoulder." Perhaps he should have paid his host a compliment, but con-
fession often follows torture: Elder had just seen the President shoot a 96.

That a President can't hold a golf club properly is not
especially surprising, for a flawed grip is shared by countless less prominent citizens. Some do it Ford's way, some
contort the left hand too far to the left and still others
strangle the club in a death grip.

Ask any ex-golfer why he quit taking lessons and he will confess that the grip "never felt right." The feeling was never right precisely because the player put feeling before function. The baseball grip—all ten fingers around the bat —feels better because of its naturalness. But in golf the grip "feels funny" at first because naturalness must be acquired. The thumbs go down the shaft, not around it, because the club needs to be guided as well as swung. In baseball, you can swing away, miss completely and you still have two more chances; in golf a missed shot counts for a stroke. The thumbs belong on the shaft because they add sensitivity to the touch.

As for the other eight fingers, two choices are available: the Vardon grip—named after Harry Vardon who won six British Opens in the days when P. G. Wodehouse's Freddie Threepwood and several unemployed butlers were the main competition—and the interlocking grip. The latter— which is used by players who have small hands—occurs when the pinky of the right hand is interlocked with the index finger of the left hand. The Vardon grip is similar except that the left index finger is kept on the club shaft, not placed over the right pinky in an overlap.

These grips may sound complicated, but they are easily understood if you have a club in hand. I have tried both grips, but prefer the interlocking, because it gives a better sense that the hands are working together: with this method I am not gripping the club as much as holding it, in much the way that I hold a steering wheel or handlebars.

With your fingers around the shaft of a golf club, indulge in some practice-range yoga and concentrate on feeling your fingertips. Forget the sensations from other parts of your body. In the swing, your arms will supply the power, but only if you have feel in your fingers can the power be controlled. When addressing the ball, look down and check the positions of your hands. If the palms are facing each other—as they should—two V's will be formed by your two thumbs and index fingers. Purists insist that both these V's should be pointing toward your rear shoulder, but it's absolutely all right to let the point of one of the V's wander a degree or two. I've been playing for years with the left V pointing toward my left shoulder and I get away with it. And you will, too; as long as your palms stay facing each other, your grip will remain balanced.

Maybe I shouldn't be getting away with that left V pointing left, but after all the hassles and frustrations I once went through to learn a correct grip, I probably should be allowed that minor break with orthodoxy. When I began golf right-handed at age eight, it "felt right" to swing at the ball cross-handed. I was attached to the cross-handed grip because it was how the hands were held in baseball when I swung left-handed, which was how my father (a Babe Ruth fan) taught me.

After a summer of this play, I noticed when caddying, that no one else had my grip. Rather than sticking stubbornly with my grip, I spent the next summer changing my hands. How awkward it felt. Yet every day I would hit one or two shots that clicked. The ball went well and my hands worked together. By the next summer playing on the little green of the four hole golf course that was our lawn, I had abandoned the cross-handed grip and, no longer thinking about it, gripped the club in the way everyone else did.

When beginning golfers tell me that it will take time to get a good feeling about their grip, I tell them to take all the time they need. It takes time for a balanced grip to feel natural. Whatever happens, don't lapse into the baseball grip. Its main flaw—aside from its never having been used by any of the game's masters—is that the hands work next to each other, not *with* each other. And that's perfectly fine for baseball, where the swing is forward only. In golf, the swing is backward and forward, and fluidity is needed more than a burst of power. Every few years, someone comes along in one of the golf magazines to tout the baseball grip, arguing, as Dave Marr did in a recent issue of *Golf Journal,* that "it's a quick and natural grip." That may be true—for hitting home runs, but not for straight drives down the fairway.

Getting a feel for a golf club can be acquired around the house. While watching TV, you can increase your pleasure by sitting in your favorite chair gripping your favorite golf club. It may look strange, but after a time it won't feel strange. And if you get to the White House and can play golf with any pros you like, it isn't likely they will later tell the world you have a poor grip on things.

Does the Ball Matter?

A Gray Goose, Futura, Spalding 75, Maxfli, PCR Bartsch, Uniroyal Super K, Winchester, Ram 3-D, Power King 80, Titleist, Zippo SDX, Jack Nicklaus, Lady PGA, Martin's VVO Scotch, Gene Littler 90, Wilson K-28, Dunlop 65, Flying Scot, Laura Baugh, Wilson Staff, All Star Super 300, Kro-Flite, Top Flite, Straight Flite, Chem Flite, Tourney, Wilson Walker Cup, Faultless, Acushnet Club Special, Jarvis Steel and Lumber, Dot, Golden Bear and Oh Shit were on sale. These golf balls, mingled among 800 others, were in the 35 cents drum at Angelo's Golf Shop on Wisconsin Avenue in northwest Washington. It's a few blocks from my home—I can reach it with a driver and eight iron —and I like to visit because Angelo Provenzano is one of the neighborhood's last craftsmen. When I bring my three

boys to the shop, I know I will be showing them both golf
and a man who is happy in his work. Angelo knows how
to convey his sense of joy, and on a practical level, he also
knows how to sell golf balls. He has five knee-high drums
marked with prices: 10 cents, 20 cents, 35 cents, 50 cents
and 90 cents.

This is the way to sell golf balls, but rarely is it the way
we are allowed to buy them. In most pro shops of the nation's 9,600 golf courses choices are limited. The show-
cases usually display Titleists, Maxflis, Top Flites, Tour-
neys, Rams, Wilson LD's or Hogans—each selling for $1.30
or $1.35. But how many non-professional golfers have $1.35
games? Most of us are in the 20 to 50 cent range.

Unless your cousin is a touring pro who gets a shipment
of 10 dozen free Titleists or Maxflis every month and
shares the spoils with you, decisions will have to be made
on how much you want to spend on golf balls. The Golf
Ball Manufacturers Association in Chicago declines to reveal the industry's annual gross, but each company stands
on its own undivoted turf and makes flashy claims for its
product. MacGregor says its Tourney has "perfect round-
ness," as if such a shape existed. Royal and Spalding Top
Flite persist in making distance claims. Both have been
running ads showing white-frocked scientists standing on
test fairways measuring the distance of balls just whacked
out at them. After its test, Royal proudly announced: "Once
again, we proved Royal is the distance champion." Spalding has laid down a $250,000 bet behind its boast that Top
Flite "is the longest ball."

Back at Angelo's, in the real world and away from the
fantasies of advertisers, the choices are simple. The 10
cent balls are the dogs, meant for the shag bag or maybe
to give to a 10-year-old who's never played before. The 20
centers are for the 90-shooters playing water holes. (That
will get their hearts pumping: gambling 20 cents they can
clear 150 yards on the fly.) The 35 cent biscuit is what you

put in your bag as a spare, for use when you've played 14 holes, lost six new balls and cry out wildly, "No more!" You'll find, using this old ball, that you will often par the last four holes.

The 50 cent lovelies at Angelo's are highly passable: name balls with only minor marks or scratches. Someone has played them perhaps a round or two before sending them over a fence or out of sight. The 90 centers, the almost new, are good enough for anyone. My own test is to hold two of them up together and drop them to the floor. If one bounces an inch or two higher, buy it. It's livelier. Don't bother about asking Angelo the difference between 80, 90 and 100 compression. He's too busy for such speculative questions, and besides no one knows much about the compression numbers except that 80 is for the bunters, 90 for the solid single swinger and 100 for the high-power hitters. Jack Nicklaus uses 100 compression balls. He said once that he uses six new balls a round. He swings so ferociously that the ball goes out of shape after a tee shot and needs three holes of rest in the caddy's pocket to regain its shape.

Golf balls are inanimate, yet I have known players who have developed emotional affiliations for one brand or another. I have had periods like this myself—when I was convinced that I would drive further if I used a Tourney, play more consistently if I hit a Wilson or more daringly with a Maxfli. How these associations get in the mind is a mystery, but one possibility is that I learned them as a boy. When I would go to golf tournaments—the Masters, the old Palm Beach round robins in the New York area, the Eastern Open in Baltimore—I would hang around the 18th green. After a player I liked holed out, I would catch him before he got to the scorer's table and ask, "Could I have your ball as a souvenir?" Most of the pros said sure and flipped me their ball. I learned that Arnold Palmer and Cary Middlecoff used Wilsons, Mike Souchak, MacGregors, Lloyd Mangrum and Shelley Mayfield, Titleists. I matched up their styles of play with the balls they used, learning years later—when other illusions passed as well —that their choice was based on what company paid them to play their ball.

For those of us who aren't paid, a 90-cent, 90-compression ball is fine. As a boy, before I went grubbing for souvenirs, I would buy one new ball a year: a cherished Silver King, a brand long extinct. I bought it in the springtime and it became my "putting ball." All of us caddies had one and we used it only on the putting greens. It was safe from losing, cutting or scuffing. Off the tees and from the fairways, we played with range balls, those red-circled rocks that wobbled out like knuckleballs when hit. But on the greens, what dignity and class we had. Today when I dream at night about golf, I am always playing a Silver King. The other afternoon at Angelo's, looking among the Gray Gooses and Kro-Flites, I would have paid 10 dollars for a 10 cent Silver King. For a little more than the price of a lesson from Angelo, I could have bought back part of my youth.

Distant Thoughts on Putting

During the past two years, my three boys, ages nine, eight and five, have learned that the putting green is the source of much of golf's excitement. And much of its mystery, because the difference between success and failure is so slight. Figuring why a putt dropped or didn't drop is often all but unfathomable. Yet they know something else—that in the choice between distance and direction, the more important is distance.

They haven't explained this in so many words. But whenever we're on the practice green they reach into my bag for the putter and go to it. The kids never take aim in any specific way. The cup is merely "over there." They talk about "how far" to hit the ball, saying, "Let's see if we can reach the hole" or "Hit it hard enough."

They've got the right idea. The greater challenge in put-ting is not precisely where to hit the ball—our eyes tell us this—but how hard. Most three-putt greens come from being too short or long on the first putt, not too wide.

How do we master the mysteries of distance? One way is the simple walk. Before putting, take yourself on a round trip between your ball and the cup. Don't make an inspection tour of it. People are behind you. Simply get the feel of the distance.

Most golfers make the mistake of spending their time lining up the putt. But what does it matter if you are a few inches this or that side of the cup? If you're on in regula-tion, and inches are the problem, you'll get your par any-way. And, if your eye is accurate, you may get a birdie.

Another way of getting close is to imagine that the hole is larger than its actual 4 1/4 inches. That near-micro-scopic smallness is enough to make anyone apprehensive. So imagine you're putting into a cup as big as a basketball hoop. Aiming into a larger area will make it easier now to measure the distance. If you are within binocular range of the cup, say 60 or 70 feet away, then imagine you are on a soccer field and you're merely trying to get the ball close to the net. (Your putt will be so long the stroke will feel like a kick.)

Many golfers address their putt with only the thought of how the ball will break in their mind. They think putting is the tricky part of the game, with all the tricks in the rolls, or what Byron Nelson calls the "underlations" of the green. But the most common cry on the greens is not "If I had just played it an inch to the left," but "Why didn't I hit it?"

If, after making the walk around your ball and the hole —quickly, you're not backpacking—and imagining you're putting into a bucket, you still can't get close, then take yourself to the practice green. That's where you should have been all along. Get a dozen balls and begin putting—

from a foot away. Don't feel embarrassed. Golf tournaments have been lost on missed one-footers. In the final round of the 1975 Hawaiian Open, Gary Groh missed a 1/4 inch putt. Still he managed to win, but only by one nervous stroke. When you can sink them all from inside one foot, move back another foot, and then another each time. This is a way to gain the kind of mental security possessed by all good putters. It is a simple truth: the more putts you sink on the practice green before play, the more confident you will be when putting during play.

P. G. Wodehouse once wrote of a supremely confident putter whose strength failed on a short putt.

Ernest Plinlimmon (in the short story, "There's Always Golf") boasted that he was "laying fifteen footers dead all the way round." But the time came on the last green one day when he "did not lay his approach putt dead. The green was one of those tricky ones. It undulated. Sometimes at the close of a tight match I have fancied that I have seen it heave, like a stage sea. Ernest putted well, but not well enough. A hummock for which he had not allowed caught the ball and deflected it, leaving him a yard and a half from the hole, that fatal distance which has caused championships to change hands.

"He shaped for the shot, however, with undiminished confidence.

" 'And now,' said Ernest Plinlimmon, 'to stuff it in.'

"His partner, who had picked up and joined us, caught my eye. He had pursed his lips gravely. He was thinking, I knew, as I was, that no good could come of this loose talk.

"Ernest Plinlimmon addressed his ball. The line was quite straight and clear, and all that was needed was the right strength. But, alas, nothing is more difficult at the end of a tense round than to estimate strength. As the ball left the clubhead, it looked to me destined for the happy ending. It trickled straight for the hole, and I was just expecting the joyful rattle which would signify that all was well, when it seemed to falter. Two feet . . . one foot . . . six inches . . . it was still moving. Three inches . . . two inches . . . I held my breath.

"Would it? Could it?

"No! Barely an inch from the cup it wavered, hesitated and stopped. He tapped it in, but it was too late. Ernest Plinlimmon had merely tied for the summer medal, and would have to undergo all the spiritual agonies of a play-off."

Even among golfers who never enter the play-offs, the agonies of the missed short putt persist. In my own game, the best way I know of assuring that this agony be kept only occasional is to tell myself just before getting over the ball, "Hit it hard enough." The reminder must be consciously repeated—on every putt. Of all the skills of the touring pros, the most obvious to those in the gallery is how strongly they putt. Only rarely do pros miss putts under 10 or 15 feet because of shortness. Instead, the putts of the pros that miss usually "slide by."

It isn't enough simply to tell yourself "Hit it hard." There remains the matter of touch. Again, it's back to the practice green. I remember one summer when I was experimenting with my game. In June, I spent two hours a day hitting with my driver and long irons. In July, those two hours were devoted to practice with middle and short irons. In August, the two hours went into putting. My scoring during August was the lowest of the summer. I averaged between 25 and 30 putts a round, and often played consecutive rounds without three-putting.

It took little more than good feeling in the hands. After so much contact with my putter, the club almost felt like an extension of my arms and fingers. By contrast, I remember what it was like another summer after I had had no contact with putting, or with any part of golf at all, for five years. On resuming play after this stretch in the desert, I was amazed to see myself hitting good drives and adequate irons. In my first reentry round, I hit 14 greens in regulation. But I took 54 putts! I four-putted five greens, three-putted eight and two-putted five. It was only after months of work on the practice green that I regained my touch.

Keeping it is the problem. There is no way to do that, except through daily golf. Because few people, aside from those on the tour or in the pages of Wodehouse, play every day, the rest of us will rarely know what it is to putt, certain that we have the touch. We are left with knowledge even a child can remember—that distance matters more than direction.

Managing the Course

Jane Blalock thought she might be about to get it going. She began her final round in the 1976 Ladies Professional Golfers Association at Pine Ridge outside of Baltimore one over par for 54 holes and four shots behind the leader. On the fifth green, she had an 18 foot putt for a birdie. She made it. That moved her up to even par, only three shots back.

For the next 12 holes, she struggled along, inching close to the leaders, Betty Burfeindt and Judy Rankin. Blalock, 31, a New Hampshire native, is a spirited and engaging woman, at ease with herself and those who come to watch her play. She has been playing professionally since 1969, has career earnings of about $300,000 and went into U.S. district court in Atlanta in 1974 to defend herself successfully against unproven accusations of cheating. Her final round at Pine Ridge, if analyzed, reveals much of the frustration and tension that professional golf—a sport of supreme loneliness—imposes on competitors. More important, it provides for the rest of us an idea or two about one of the least teachable aspects of golf—managing the course. Whether this involves being able to concentrate for several hours straight, consistently avoiding trouble, or playing your own game regardless of the opposition, managing the course means that a continuity of control exists between the first drive on No. 1 to the final putt on 18.

Taking the momentum of the birdie on the fifth, Blalock scored another on the seventh. When she came to the eighth hole, a par three over water that is a harder test than it looks, she hit a middle iron to about 30 feet to the right. The ball rested on the fringe, with a sloping downhill putt. In fear of sliding it past, she left her putt three feet short. Some pros call the three-footer the most treacherous shot in golf, because it demands the most sensitivity and because it is so heartbreaking when missed. Blalock, playing a break that wasn't there, missed it.

It was a moment to cave in. But she went to the next hole —a par five—and played two wood shots and a wedge to 20 feet. She made the putt. At the end of nine, she had picked up another stroke and was now only two shots behind. What Blalock did on the front nine displayed course management at its most skilled: she stuck to the fairway, played to the middle of the greens except where sticking it close involved little risk, and avoided letting the three-putt green get to her.

On the back nine, she scored pars on 10, 11 and 12, then ran in a 50 foot birdie putt at 13, a long and difficult dogleg that few other women were pouncing on. She came to the 14th knowing it was an easy par three—over water but to a wide and reachable green. The emotions, like the muscles, need a rest, but in golf the temptation is to think that an easy shot means easing up. To everyone's astonishment, she pulled her drive far left, between some pines and behind the gallery. When she got to her ball, she saw that she had about 20 feet of green to work with but some 30 feet of frog hair and mud to get over. She could either run the ball to the green or pitch it. At first, she chose to pitch, then she changed her mind. No, she had another thought. Then still another. Finally, she took a four iron and gave it a punch that was meant to run the ball through the grass and mud. It didn't, of course. The ball fell short of the green and Blalock was forced to struggle for a bogey while her playing partners scored easy pars.

The next hole saw her save a par. After a poor approach and a feeble chip, she sank a 20-footer for a par in an example of the perky courage that makes Blalock one of the more exciting players in golf. Then she came to another easy hole. After a straight drive and deft approach, she missed a four foot straight-in putt and took a par. Still alive, she did what no one expected: on the demanding 17th, a par three from a high tee to a narrow green with water on the left and a trap on the right, she birdied. Now she needed one more birdie on the easy par five 18th to bring her in at three under. That would be a 69 and, if Burfeindt bogied one of her last three holes, that would earn her a tie and a play-off.

Two routine wood shots put her in front of the green, with only a half-wedge to a slightly elevated green. Instead of taking advantage of another routine shot, she left it about 40 feet short, then three-putted for a six.

That gave her a 71 for a 291 total, which put her four strokes back, exactly where she had begun the day. The round was tormenting because her mistakes had come from forgetting the fundamentals on the easy shots: get the ball up to the hole, keep it in play, go for the center of the green.

Course management involves the fundamentals, if nothing else. It leaves players open to good scoring if they can get hot but it doesn't cast them into dungeons if they can't. In Blalock's round, she was able to get hot, but the trouble was she couldn't keep her game merely warm when warm was all she needed. She managed the course deftly for 14 holes, but for four holes—the easiest ones—she neutralized all the gains she made.

After turning in a 71, and knowing she'd failed, Blalock sat dejected with friends near the clubhouse. But her lamentations were brief. When leaving the grounds in a car driven by a friend, she jumped out and rode down the long driveway on the hood. She smiled to the crowds, joked with the cops as they tried to unjam the traffic and was much the image of a woman who, unfazed by defeat, felt good about herself. After opening rounds of 75 and 74 put her in 23rd place and seven shots behind the leaders, she came close to winning. More important than coming close was that she had come back.

Stay-at-home Golf

It has happened to all of us. We are leaving the house for the golf course when our non-golfing neighbors spot us, saying they'd like to come along sometime: "We've always wanted to play golf—and it's about time we started."

Be grateful they said "sometime." They could have wanted to come along today. Yet the problems of the aspiring golfers must be faced; no broom of evasiveness can permanently brush them off.

What your neighbors need to be told, first, is that no one learns golf on the golf course. That's where the game is played. The place to send future golfers—if they have the successful execution of some golf shots in mind—is not the fairways but their own backyards. Give them an old club, say a five iron, and tell them to spend the next few days making its acquaintance.

Five irons, like many strangers, are hard to get to know. In golf, feeling counts more than muscle, timing more than strength, rhythm more than power. The golf swing, to be effective, should become as much a habit as possible, which means that you don't want to be bothered thinking about it every time. Enough other distractions will always be present. In their back yards, your swinging neighbors will be able to get some idea of whether or not they have the feeling, timing and rhythm to have a wild chance of enjoying the game. Low scoring is certainly not the object at first; enjoyment is. If you take prospective golfers out to the course with no preparation for the humiliation and torment that awaits them, they will be victimized by the severest of fates: pressured to quit while they are behind.

Take them to the course only after they've had at least eight hours—an honest day's labor—of swinging a club. Never mind that they haven't been hitting a ball at home, much less aiming it at a target. By practicing first in the back yard and getting somewhat familiar with the habit of swinging the club, the chances are much better of their hitting a few modestly decent shots the first time out. I have never taken anyone to the golf course for the first time who didn't express amazement at the awesome physical breadth of the acreage. To the unfocused eye, the size has to be intimidating. Taking hopeful golfers to 150 to 200 acres of earth, unarmed with even an idea of how they are going to get around it, is to risk letting them be all but swallowed up by their own insignificance.

What might make the difference is the idea or two they have developed about the golf swing. Nothing is less obvious. In the drawings of cavemen, we always see them swinging their clubs at other cavemen's heads or chests. The target is eye level. In golf, the target is some five or six feet below eye level, depending on one's height. What this means, as we roam the fairways delighting in how we have evolved from the Neanderthals, is that swinging a golf club is neither instinctual nor natural. If the game were the latter, the tee would be five or six feet high.

Not long ago, I was playing with a man who, in understandable rage at three-putting from six feet, picked his ball out of the cup, tossed it in the air, swung mightily—with the putter no less—and creamed the ball 200 yards. It was his most solid shot of the day, the direction aside. It was because the ball was before his eyes when he swung. His swing was a wholly natural effort.

If your neighbors have found pleasure in the dry runs of back yard swinging and have grown only more eager for the challenge of the course, make a few observations. Check their practice swings. Are they jerky or smooth? Do they grip the club as though it's a weapon or a tool? On the backswing, do they lurch off toward the rear fence, or do they appear to have their arms working together? These are points to note. If the results are positive, take them to the course sometime. If not, pass along the advice Sam Snead gave to someone who assuredly wasn't going to make it: "Lay off for three weeks and then quit for good."

Go Around in Circles

Golf is a game of circles: standing on a round planet, hitting a round ball into a round hole and tromping around in circles doing it. But the most crucial circle of all is the one a player makes during the swing. Or should make. Most golfers, bubbling like samovars, explode at the ball and forget, in the heat, to swing in a circular arc. On the backswing, they pick up the club and then chop at the ball on the downswing. Or they drag the club back slowly and lift it to the topswing, then spring downward like a butcher knifing into a beef shank.

The circular swing is one in which the arms, not the wrists, control the action. Before taking the clubhead back, nestle it closely to the ball—not touching but close, with little space in between. From there, the arms should sweep the club back, low along the ground. The club will pick up by itself, from the natural extension of the arms and the turning of the shoulders. If you jerk the club or lift it with the wrists, the arc of the swing will be destroyed. Instead of a full backswing, you will have a wristy one. The power of the golf swing should not be decentralized, especially not to such a joint as the wrist during the backswing. The wrists coordinate the strength of the hands and arms, but their place in the swing comes later —in the downswing.

As you sweep the club back, you achieve the most celebrated position in golf: the straight forward arm. People who never play golf and don't know the difference between a tee marker and a ball washer, are usually familiar with the legendary sacredness of the straight left arm. Brendan Gill's *Here At The New Yorker* includes a photograph of a staff writer teeing off; the notes and comment of the caption single out for praise the gentleman's straight left arm. The physics of the unbent left elbow mean nothing more than that the circle of the swing has been kept intact. The club can't be moved out of the proper arc if the left arm stays firm.

At the top of the swing, the force of momentum precludes any chance for reflection. It is too late to think. I have played with those who paused on the topswing. Claude Harmon was one. But I can think of no other professional who did. Pausing during the swing creates an unnatural break in rhythm. The motion of the club should be smooth and simple: sweep it back, bring it down. The pull downward needs to follow the path of circularity, or else the club will hack down on the ball, and a topped, smothered or dribbled shot will result. To hit the ball solidly, the clubface must be brought to the point of impact with a movement of purity in the cleanliness of the arc.

As your ball sits on the tee or turf awaiting the impact of your swing, your right arm should dominate the downswing. Forget about the straight forward arm at this point. Your wrists are about to cock, and they should be ready to receive the full strength of your rear arm. Some of the playing pros talk about the power of the forward arm, and that is how they hit those majestic shots that scream out low, rise high, hang for a moment in the air and float to the ground. But for most of us our stronger arm is to the rear. That's our arm that supplies the power. Use it.

When you strike the ball, your swing is only two-thirds complete: backswing and downswing. Unless the club continues on in the circle you have created, the ball may still go anywhere. The follow-through is crucial because it provides direction to sweep the club through to the target. As a result, the ball has a better chance of going there. And so do you, rather than heading off for a tramp in the woods.

None of the mechanics of the swing is even close to being simple. But the problems of the swing should not be added to. A main distraction is the waggle. Rather than beginning the swing by beginning the swing, the waggler moves into action by twitching. It can be a muscle movement in the left leg, a forward press of the hands, a quick shift of the feet (the Billy Casper waggle) or a wiggle in the rear end (the Sam Snead waggle). I knew a golfer in college who did a disguised jug before swinging. In time, his waggling became so pronounced that he needed a mini-waggle as a booster thrust to get into his maxi-waggle.

Mini or maxi, the waggle is useless. And it's addictive. If you want to quit, you can approach it gradually on the practice tee. Address the ball and leave the clubface resting on the ground behind the ball. Think of the moment as one of repose. The ball is still, the clubface is still, your body is still. Then begin the swing. Take the club back directly—that's the only kind of preparation you actually need.

45 ·

Keep the Rules and
They Keep You

Forty-one rules aren't so many—St. Benedict had 73 to keep the brethren on the straight and narrow. Yet, many golfers who have mastered the runics of the swing have not bothered much to master the simplicities of the rules, kept current by the vigilant fathers of the United States Golf Association and the Royal and Ancient Golf Club of St. Andrews, Scotland.

Most golfers are quite content with a mere acquaintance of the few basics that keep the game civilized—no kicking your opponent's ball into the rough when he's not looking, no stealing the honor on the tee—but after that, it often seems that anything goes. This attitude of abandon is more fitting for sports in which blood lust is an asset—like sparring with broken pool cues. Golf courses are havens for the non-hostile, where umpires and referees are not needed because the players themselves know the rules and obey them.

Is there a finer joy, short of clearing a pond by inches, than assessing an opponent two strokes who (as though playing croquet) strikes your ball on the putting green (breaching rule 35), cleans a muddy ball on the fairway (violating rule 23) or marks a line of flight on a blind shot over a hill (breaking rule 9)?

When calling attention to these rules and their unpleasant penalties, be prepared for pouting or fuming. You will be accused of unmentionable practices. But think of yourself, at such times, as Abraham Lincoln walking back those 10 miles (a distance somewhat exceeding 27 holes of golf) to return the penny. Your mission is honesty.

When someone tells you that you lead a dull life, deep in the sopor of rules and laws, tell them Arnold Palmer probably won the 1958 Masters because he knew the rules. On the par three 12th hole of the final round, on a soggy day in Augusta, Palmer flew the green and the ball imbedded in the back apron. A dispute arose when Palmer claimed he was entitled to a free drop; the official in the green jacket said no. Each was satisfied when Palmer played both a provisional ball, on which he scored three, and his first ball, on which he took a five. The tournament rules men then huddled and determined that Palmer was entitled to a free drop and the three stood.

If the alertness of a Palmer is not sufficiently instructive, consider the wisdom of P. G. Wodehouse, who seldom broke 110. In one of his golf fables, Joseph Poskitt was playing Wadsworth Hemmingway for the President's Cup. On the ninth hole, over water, Poskitt hit one of his "colossal drives." He started to leave the tee but Hemmingway said, "One moment," and asked, "Are you not going to drive?"

" 'Don't you call that a drive?' Poskitt replied.

47 ·

" 'I do not. A nice practice shot, but not a drive. You took the honor when it was not yours. I, if you recollect, won the last hole. I am afraid I must ask you to play again.'

" 'What?'

" 'The rules are quite definite on this point,' said Hemmingway, producing a well-thumbed volume . . .

"Poskitt returned to the tee and put down another ball. There was a splash. 'Playing three,' said Hemmingway. Poskitt drove again. 'Playing five,' said Hemmingway.

" 'Must you recite?' said Poskitt.

" 'There is no rule against calling the score.'

" 'I concede the hole,' said Poskitt."

I had a similar experience once, playing with Bobby Riggs, who knew the rules were there as much for his advantage as for orderly play. We were playing a course on Long Island, when on the first hole I happened to tee my ball ahead of the markers—by a matter of inches. The moment before my backswing, Riggs called out, "Wait!" Startled, I paused mid-swing. He sprung to the left marker, pulled it from the ground and moved it ahead by about a foot. "There," he said. "Swing away. You're behind the markers now." It was a subtle move and totally unnerving. My feelings were so vacillating between wonder at his nerve and rage that I sent my drive out of bounds. Riggs won the hole.

The St. Andrew's Scots who wrote the early rules were Calvinists who believed that although a golf course may look like paradise its users are potential wrong doers. Shadows of sneakiness loom in us all, however sunny an aspect we present on the first tee. What is to prevent, say, a threesome of professionals from rigging their scores by signing cards two or three strokes lower than their actual tallies? Strikingly, it has always been one of the game's distinctions that the golf tour has never had a major cheating scandal. In 1972 Jane Blalock was accused of moving her ball in the rough by some other women on the tour, but the charges were never proven. In fact, she sued, in turn, the Ladies Professional Golfers Association and won a judgment that the LPGA was in violation of the Sherman Antitrust Act for not allowing her to compete in tournaments while her case was pending. In amateur golf, only the Deepdale scandal of the mid-1950s (in which phony handicaps were used by some of the contestants) is a splotch on the sport's purity. I have played with board members of corporations who lied, stole and cheated their way to the top, but who on the fairways were watchful of golf's rules and its etiquette.

Watchfulness goes to the heart of the matter, or at least to the aorta. It is not a great strain, for example, to avoid walking in the line of another's putt. Small effort is needed to keep from moving behind a player as he addresses the ball. And only moderate self-control is required to refrain from hitting into the foursome ahead. All that these standards of basic etiquette ask is that we simply be watchful of the other player, so that what we do on the golf course doesn't make it harder for our partners.

As a boy, I made a point of learning the rules. I would study them in the caddy yard while waiting to be assigned a loop. And, indeed, how often I came to use them. During the course of a round, I would watch closely whoever had matches against those I was caddying for. When I saw a violation, I would call aside my employer and tell him what his opponent had just done. Usually, my man would be glad to get the facts and take action. Occasionally, though, my information was rejected. It would be too embarrassing, some thought. Others feared a stink. Some doubted that the rules made sense. But these were the exceptions. In time, I came to be sought out as a caddy, because my services went beyond merely carrying the clubs and attending the pin. They went directly to the heart of the game—the rules.

It is not by accident that the rules discuss "courtesy on

49   ·

the course" at the top of Section One. When golfers join private country clubs, and fork over high sums for initiation fees and monthly dues, invariably they talk with relief about no longer having to endure public course etiquette. They have something there: behavior on the nation's municipal and public fairways often makes a Route 66 truck stop seem like a well-mannered salon. In the past two decades, many of those taking up the game have been ruffians and rowdies. My suspicions are that golf began attracting the ruck when Arnold Palmer came along. Sitting on the barstools and looking blearily at the corner TV, the unrefined saw Palmer as their model. His thick neck, slashing swing and bullish play became the lightning rod down which the electrified masses slid on their way to the clubhouse. Many brought their rowdiness with them. If they take it any place else, it is when they walk behind the ropes at a tournament in Arnie's Army. There, among shouting and shoving, crudeness and incivility rank high, as General Arnie is cheered on. Pros find it difficult to be paired with Palmer, for he attracts the rabble for whom etiquette, if they know the term at all, connotes questionable chromosomes. Palmer himself is often victimized by his own enthusiasts. I have seen him playing wretched golf only to walk the fairways thick with fans calling out, "Go get 'em, Arnie," when all he is capable of getting at that point is another struggle for par.

The point at which many golfers walk away from the rules is when they opt for preferred lies. The advantages of winter rules were intended to apply only when the earth is craggy, pocked by the harshness of the cold and other rudenesses of the winter weather. Such conditions rarely prevail mid-summer. Yet, the winter rules player counters that golf is hard enough without enduring the torment of uncivil real estate; if your Titleist lands in a vulgar piece of turf, move it to a more chaste spot. But rule 16 applies in all seasons: "The ball shall be played as it lies and shall not be purposely touched except that the player may, without penalty, touch his ball with his club in the act of addressing it and except as otherwise provided in the rules of local rules."

The challenge of accepting whatever lie we get is fundamental to the pleasures of golf. To accept the rub of the green, even when we must cross it against the grain, is to bring an objectivity to our play that refreshes the spirit. Once when I had the miffy luck of landing a tee shot in a divot hole, my companion called out, "Move the ball, it's OK. When I land in a divot I'll move mine." How tempting it was—to nudge the ball an inch or two to a tuft of grass waiting since the fourth day of creation for a golf ball to land. But who needs to go easy on themselves while at play? By accepting the conditions of turf on the fairways, you gather respect for yourself. When someone tells you, "Move the ball, it's only a game," answer, "No thanks." It's because golf *is* a game that we can accept its full reality.

In the end, some will always take the preferred lie, as others will ignore the sanctions of other rules. Fidelity to the rules is an acquired skill, and only the few who work at it experience its pleasures. For those who wish to bend the rules, there are always those putt-putt courses next to the truck stops. There, they can shout and stomp until their larynxes loosen when they miss that 10-footer off the sideboard. Amid the traffic and fumes, what could be more appropriate.

Divotology

In the summers during college when I worked as a greenskeeper,* I learned that, despite land abuse, divot-making
had to be tolerated. The major irritation came in seeing so
many well-intentioned golfers persisting in the myth that
you should always replace your divot. Strong evidence ex-
ists that when the turf flies, the universe, the fairway and
your conscience may be better served by not replacing the
divot. It isn't at all certain that the replaced divot will ever
grow again, however fervently your reclamation program
may be; the strip-mined site sometimes should be left that

*The 6 P.M. to 3 A.M. watering shift at the North Shore Country
Club, Glen Head, New York, $1.50 an hour with all the putting by
moonlight I wanted.

way, its original contour to be restored by the greenskeepers.

As a gesture of civility to those playing behind you, that day or that year, replacing the divot has merit, if only to keep someone from having to play out of your pothole. But courtesy aside, what you need to know is the kind of grass on which you are playing. According to the Golf Course Superintendents Association, 46 percent of the courses in America are bluegrass, 22 percent bent and 22 percent Bermuda. The remaining 10 percent, apparently, are mixed, which means they are pastures lucky to be mowed, let alone categorized. If you don't know what kind of grass is growing under your feet, ask the pro.

If you are playing on Bermuda, it is definitely useless to replace your divot. The grass has underground stems (rhizomes) that recuperate quickly and viridly. Bermuda lets Mother Nature, the great lady of the fairways, replace the divots. She has never missed a one on Bermuda. On bent or bluegrass fairways, replaced divots may grow back in the spring or fall, though summertime growth is questionable. Even under the best of conditions, only the attentively replaced divot has a chance of surviving. Instead of merely tamping the turf into the excavation, the conscientious golfer will mat it down with tees—one inserted at the front of the divot, the other in the back, the way club sandwiches are held together in restaurants where they cost $4 apiece. Stitched surgically by tees, the replaced patch of turf will not be scuffed away when the fairway mowing and fertilizing machines roll over it. The respected superintendent at the Columbia Country Club, in Chevy Chase, Maryland, George Thompson, acknowledges that many greenskeepers prefer to reseed divot holes themselves, lest the replaced turf fails to take and the scars become permanent. A few times a month, one of Thompson's crew will be sent out on reseeding expeditions, beginning at the front of the first fairway and working around to the end of the 18th.

Knowing the appropriate agronomics is a saddleweight that often rests heavy. On Bermuda courses, I have found myself pressed on occasion to explain to playing partners and caddies why I don't replace my divots; on bent or bluegrass courses I am seen as eccentric when I secure the replaced turf by sticking tees through it. Sometimes, in explaining myself but feeling I'm not getting through, I quote John Muir on reverence for the land or refer my golf partners to Aldo Leopold's classic work, *Sand County Almanac.* If my own concentration is broken by the burden of knowing too much about divots, it also works the other way. I have unnerved many an opponent not only by failing to recycle my divot but by stepping up to it and swinging at it with my club, obliterating the turf so that no one can replace it.

Left intact, the divot can be a useful source of information about your swing. A few years ago, when most of my irons were going left—either as pulls or outright hooks— I analyzed every part of my game in an attempt to figure out the flaw. Hands, shoulder turn, hips—none of them, when I watched closely, offered a clue. The discovery came when I flew an eight iron far to the left of the green. Instead of walking on, I looked down and noticed the divot hole. It was a dogleg left. The clubhead was coming in from the outside. The ball had no chance to go straight. After the round, I hit about a hundred balls, thinking of nothing except digging out a straight divot mark. The turf was flying and flying well. I was little concerned about the flight of the ball. That can take care of itself. I stopped my leftward drift and have been hitting straight divots since.

The truest friend of the earth, among sporting enthusiasts, assuredly, is one who does not dig at all. But that isn't golf. Precision iron play occurs when the ball is hit on the last finely split-second of the downswing. There occurs one of the least natural aspects of golf: hitting down at the ball to make it go up. Yet it is so. On the tour, few execute a better divot than Lee Trevino. A stylish divot, such as the kind Trevino gets off, is one that floats through the air, hovers aloft a second and drops softly. It should travel from 15 to 20 feet.

Selecting the Perfect Pro

What if an imaginative friend gives you a birthday gift of five lessons with the pro of your choice? Which pro would you choose?

To begin with, look for a professional who is free of theories. Theorists care only for their own convenience: It is easier to fit you to their theories than to take the trouble to figure out exactly what's wrong with your game or what needs developing. I know of many men and women who now trudge in anguish upon the scorched fairways of Living Hell Country Club only because their games were ruined by a theoretician. One pro believes the right hand is everything, another talks of nothing but the shoulder turn. Still others swear by left side action, or by hip movement or by the still head.

But what if your hands, shoulders, hips and head are not the problem. Theorists will never tell you because they are tied to their formulas, made pat by years of repetition. Golf pros can't be sued for malpractice when they butcher your golf game, so ask around about a few pros before letting one practice surgery on your swing. If a pro is a theorist, stay away.

Perceptive pros go to the teaching tee resigned to the failing ways of man. The offenses they are about to see you commit, as you hit a few, will try their patience and stupefy their spirit; but a measure of empathy will get them through it all. They know you are taking a lesson with hopeful expectations. The empathetic pros will be hopeful, too, slaving away for 60 minutes because they believe you can be taught the fundamentals.

Touring pros often tell us about when their games went sour and they slinked home for a lesson from a club pro who knew them on their way up. When Tom Watson had putting troubles, he sought out former PGA champion Jerry Barber; soon after he came out of his putting slump, and finished second the next week in the 1976 Los Angeles Open. "I have to give Barber credit for all those birdies I made," admitted Watson. "I was standing on my right side too much, putting too much weight on that side, and had my left shoulder too high." Dave Hill sought his friend Deane Beman. Frank Beard looked up Paul Runyan. Jane Blalock went to Bob Toski. Jack Nicklaus called in Jack Grout.

The return of these prodigals is always to fundamentals. Thousands of styles of golf swings can be found, but there is only one set of fundamentals. Pros with empathy will explain them to us, realizing that their efforts will likely go for nothing. We will continue to slice, hook, dribble and foozle. Pros who lack empathy will take our continued hacking personally. They shouldn't. They ought to console us for our straying ways, not rebuke us. The tender word, not the sharp word, does better for us.

If your pro passes both tests, thank the angels. If the pro mumbles, forgets your name, drops big names, spends half your lesson hitting your balls, well, try to be empathetic yourself. Club pros have no picnic. Every member is their boss, they have to work weekends, when they shoot an 81 in the weekly pro-am the caddies snicker, they must be glamorous and heroic to the members, fatherly to the juniors, wary with the salesmen, scraping to the greens committee and dutifully chivalrous to the bores forever hanging around the pro shop asking questions about swing weight, speculating on who will be the next Nicklaus or whether Titleists go further than Maxflis.

With all that awaiting them every morning, it's not surprising than an occasional teaching pro desires to emulate Ben Hogan. As the story goes, Gary Player once placed a trans-Atlantic call to Fort Worth, where Hogan manufactures golf clubs. When Player asked for a lesson over the phone, Hogan asked Player whose clubs he used on the tour. Dunlop, Player replied. Then go get a lesson from Mr. Dunlop, Hogan snapped, and hung up.

There are teaching pros with similar temperament. Considering that most of the people they instruct never apply themselves to practicing what was just taught, it is a justified mood. But except for a few permanent cranks, most teaching professionals come to the golf course running strong with hope in the thought that no sporting union is better than a human being and a golf course.

Patience and the Par Five

Par fives currently enjoy a good press. It is rare to read the paper on Monday and not learn how a tournament was turned around the day before by a final round eagle. That was how Bruce Lietzke won the 1977 Hawaiian Open. Needing a par on the 73rd hole, 566 yards, he cranked a four iron to the green and sunk the putt to win by three shots over Don January. Sometimes, pros *begin* with eagles—as did Laura Baugh on the par five first hole of the 1976 Ladies Professional Golf Championship in Baltimore. At the 1975 Greensboro tournament, Tom Weiskopf reached one par five with an eight iron second shot. In the final round of the same tournament, Lee Elder drove on a par five and holed out his second shot with a five iron. Slowly, we have gotten it into our heads that getting home in two is routine.

The wiser golfer knows that the way to master par fives has little to do with what happens on the first or second shot. A routine drive and a workable second shot will do. If both are executed only moderately well, then the odds increase for an easy third shot into the green. If that shot is flubbed, it's still possible to save par with a recovery shot. But what if, in straining to overpower your drive, you overbear it instead, sending it 100 feet into the woods instead of 100 yards up the fairway? You are in for a likely six or a seven.

On the second shot, the birdie temptation grows even greater. It may be possible at that point to see the green. We begin to lust: we can get there in two. When we swing, we wind ourselves into painful contortions. Statistics are needed for confirmation, but probably more mistakes are made on the second shots of par fives than on any other strokes for those long holes. I know this is true for myself and for most of those I play with or watch in tournaments.

Talk to Sam Snead about par fives. He needed a routine par five to win the 1939 U. S. Open. Instead of a five, he took an eight, finished in a blaze of ignominy and lost by two shots. Snead would probably give a good share of his fortune today for that par, because he never won the Open— a fact that most golfers remember about him.

Patience and restraint—virtues that would seem endemic to golfers in the first place (we are neither among the world's hurried nor harried)—should be in our hearts when we approach par fives. We need not face a par five in nervousness and trembling. Save that for the water holes. The strategy of the par five is to keep the options open as long as possible—with a medium drive and a fair second shot. Then it is time to assess the situation and judge whether you have something dramatic to go for or not.

An unusual solution for dealing with the par five has been provided by Walter O'Malley, the owner of the Los

Angeles Dodgers. He built his own course in Vero Beach, Florida, where his team takes spring training. It is a challenging and refreshing layout, and I have played it often, sometimes with good results. The most enchanting part of the Dodgertown course is the 680 yard third hole. It is so long—more than a third of a mile—that O'Malley saw no reason to lure golfers into trying too hard for a par five. He made the hole a par six.

Controlling the Tantrum
with Bolt's Law

One of the more fearless acts of my 30 years in golf came when, as an innocent of 16, I caddied for Tommy Bolt. It was in 1954 at the Palm Beach Round Robin, a tournament sponsored by the clothing company and which was played that year at the old Meadowbrook course in Westbury, Long Island. Bolt was four years away from winning the U. S. Open at Tulsa, but already he had a national reputation: for his temper. The press had a string of nicknames for him: Terrible Tommy, Tantrum Tom, Thunder Bolt. Stories in the caddy yard were told of his fits and outbursts. He threw clubs into the ground with such downward velocity that two caddies were sometimes needed to tug them out of the earth. The snapped club shaft over his knee was often the mildest form of his rage. The depths of golf course lakes, from Pebble Beach to Montauk Point, were littered with barnacled clubs sent to the bottom by Bolt. When he three-putted a green and went to the next tee, no tree in his path was safe from having a putter wrapped around its trunk. On occasion, Bolt would retreat into the woods and pound his driver into the earth, calling out to the clubhead a list of oaths and curses to justify the beating. It was avenger Tom Bolt meting out a sentence of physical punishment to a golf club guilty of the criminal act of three-putting.

"You want to caddy for that guy?" was the reaction when I talked of my ambitions to work for Bolt. Being known in my neighborhood for softness in taking in stray cats and befriending the kids that the rest of the class maltreated, my preference for the crazy Bolt was seen as another aberration. I had my chance to satisfy it on the Tuesday before the tournament began. It was five in the afternoon, and the day was slowing down. Some of the other players in the 16-man field were coming in from practice rounds. My hope was not so lofty as caddying for Tommy Bolt, because the caddy master would hardly give his bag to a kid of 16 when the yard was filled with experienced year-round caddies. But by five in the afternoon, none of the veterans was around. They had left for the day or were still on the course.

It was then that Bolt drove into the Meadowbrook parking lot, visible from the caddy yard. I ran to his car and was there to take his clubs as he opened the trunk. "Thanks, son," said Tom. "We've got time for about 12 holes." I didn't know what Bolt meant until I realized that he thought I had been assigned to caddy for him. "Yeah, Mr. Bolt, just about 12 holes," I said. I was all but overcome by the vapors. My scrapbook at home was fat with clippings of Bolt victories along the tour, and here he was about to entrust his fortunes to me. While Bolt went to the clubhouse to change, I went to the first tee. I avoided going past the caddy master because he would have taken away my loop and given it to one of the regulars.

In a few minutes, Bolt came out and we were off. "We." Caddies use that term because many of them insist—as well as do many of the pros whose equipment and ego they carry—that a team is formed. Although it was a total illusion in the case of Bolt and me, it was a high moment to be in the personal employ of a living legend. All notions of his supposedly uncontrollable rage vanished, because I was seeing Bolt as the stylish and disciplined athlete he truly was. His swing had the smooth flow of power and timing that—to my mind—only Snead, Nelson, Littler and a few others have ever achieved. His iron shots were hit down and through, with the ball being floated more than hit.

We went 12 holes. Rather than being the monster he was made out to be, Bolt was a kindly and gentle man. He talked about his own boyhood in Oklahoma and he asked about mine. He dispensed the routine advice—"Stay in school, son"—and sighed that being a touring pro was a gypsy life that only the driven nomads should pursue. As for his temper, he allowed that although he should be the last one to preach or sermonize on temper control, he believed he knew the secret for playing calm golf. In an Oklahoma drawl, he explained: "Ever' time afore Old Tom goes out to play, I tell myself I'm goin' to miss at least six shots this round. When I miss 'em, I don't get mad. I knew aforehand."

Bolt's theory about temper control has remained with me over the years. I have heard others lay claim to it, and perhaps he picked it up from others before him, but I credit him with it, if only because few others have been as tormented on the course by the difficulties of self-control. He knew what it was to fall and rise again, so his method, I thought, deserved respect.

Bolt's estimate of six missed shots per round is about

what the professionals must endure. That's roughly nine percent of their shots, if they shoot, say, a 70. I would estimate that the number of missed shots doubles for every 10 shots: the 80-shooter botches about 12 times a round, the 90-shooter 24 times, the 100-shooter, forget it. When about to lose your temper, because you lipped a two-foot putt, skulled a wedge out of a trap across the green or skied a tee shot, remember where the error originated. In team sports, your flubs can be dumped on your teammates' ineptitude, but in golf you are the entire team.

It doesn't make sense to imagine you can ignore your temper. It's part of you. Golf would be temperamentally more simple if such animal activities as jumping, kicking or throwing were involved. Who knows whether a football player who hits the line hard is throwing a skilled block or a tantrum? In tennis, the smash may be a scarcely disguised release of frustration. In baseball, Billy Martin has agitated the fans for years by mouthing off at umpires, while many a sportswriter has called him "scrappy." In golf Martin would have been suspended from the tour for talking like that, even to himself.

We lose our temper on the golf course not because the results shame us but because we weren't emotionally prepared for them. This doesn't mean you should murmur to yourself before each shot, "I'll probably hook, slice, shank, or chilly-dip," but only that you should be ready for something less than perfection. Such is the pain of a flopped shot: we see the laurel wreath drop from the heroic figures we secretly imagine ourselves. Uncrowned we stand after a missed one-footer. The tantrum—heaving a club at a tree, pounding the clubhead into the turf, ramming the club into the bag (watch Weiskopf do that when he takes a six)—is a psychological defense against what we think is an undeserved injustice. We merit far better than this punishment from the gods, we reason, so a little storm will set heaven straight. In the area of temper control, the choice is keeping yourself either free of wrath or free of illusions—that you are better than other mortals and therefore deserve better breaks. The path free of illusion is the easier route.

When you blow up, be assured that although the members of your foursome appear to look away as you slam your putter against your shoe—and perhaps miss that shot, too, cracking your ankle bone—they are actually looking on. If they have a bet of a few dollars, or their own illusions, riding on the round, they can't help but wonder how your blowup will affect your game. For some, one tantrum ruins the whole round. For others, losing control has only a temporary effect.

The logical way to achieve temper control is to hit fewer shots that are upsetting. But that is too lofty a goal. When Joann Carner or Lee Trevino miss a shot, they have a right to explode—because they have done so often perfectly what they just did imperfectly. But the rest of us have little choice but accept ourselves and our emotions the way they are. If you must, shout and curse at yourself *before* you get to the course for all the shots you will miss after you tee off. Then when you do miss them—remember Bolt's Law —stay calm. Take it from someone who knew.

Sandslicing

Coming out of the sand, Walter Hagen believed, should be the easiest of all golf shots: It is the only one in which the ball isn't hit. It's the sand you strike.

That may explain the uncertainties suffered by most golfers in a bunker. How do you hit a few thousand grains of sand so that they, in turn, propel a golf ball and move it up, out and, hopefully, close? A golfer, taking a wedge in hand and going into a bunker feels like Antoine de Saint-Exupéry in the buoyant classic, *Wind, Sand and Stars:* "I walked to the top of a sandhill and looked around the horizon like a captain on his bridge. This sea of sand bowled me over. Unquestionably it was filled with mystery and danger."

Saint-Exupéry was speaking of the great desert of North

Africa, but the little Saharas in front of the greens, those at the sides of the fairway and those midway between tee and green that innocently catch your weak second shot, have mysteries and dangers of their own. As if bunker play weren't already uniquely difficult—hitting the sand, not the ball—it's doubly so because you cannot ground the club. Rule 33 on hazards expressly forbids that; you may bring it as close to the sand as you wish and wave it as mystically as your inner voice directs, but touch a grain and it is a stroke penalty. About all rule 33 allows you to do in a sand hazard is stand in it.

The stance is a fair place to begin. Dig yourself in. Sinking firmly down will also give you a fix on the texture of the sand: is it firm, coarse, flaky, wet or loose? With this knowledge, you'll have some idea of where to hit the sand behind the ball. The delicacy of the trap shot comes in exploding the sand in a way that the ball is neither skulled across the green—like the doomed stroke of Jack Nicklaus on one of the closing holes in the 1975 Open at Medinah—or fluffed out weakly, like the Lou Graham shot on the 72nd hole of the same tournament.

The finesse of the bunker shot comes from slicing (rather than blasting) into the sand. A blast requires one major exertion of force which often, when the exertion stops, causes the sand to splash further out of the trap than the ball. Slicing into the sand is only the beginning—you should also slice out of it. Examine the sand trap pictures that sports editors love to run—lots of action in all those sand particles coming at the camera—and you will see a full follow-through by the golfer. It is deliberate. Because the ball comes out of the sand slower and softer than the ordinary fairway shot takes to the air, the clubhead must stay with the ball longer. The geometry of all the angles is not as important as remembering to swing the club *through* the sand. With an open stance, you should deliberately move the club in the direction of the hole, after impact.

On the backswing, the usual full arc is not needed. Instead, pick the club up quickly, especially if you need to get over a high lip. Remember the seven Johnny Miller took on the par three seventh hole at Winged Foot in 1974? He hit into the deep trap to the left of the green and needed three tries to get it out. I was in the gallery behind him that day and could have told him he needed more chop and less sweep in his backswing. The same was true for Betty Burfeindt at the 1976 Girl Talk Classic at Wykagyl in Westchester County, New York. She took four tries to get out of a trap in one of the early holes in the last round. If she could have gotten out, and down in only two putts, she would have won the tournament.

Professionals enjoy theorizing about bunker play, perhaps because getting out of the sand is easier to talk about than do. But professional advice is often conflicting. In *Tips From the Teaching Pros* (Harper & Row, 1969), Buck Worsham tells us on page 120 how to hit a trap shot: "Look at the back of the ball instead of one or two inches behind it." Turn the page, and there's his brother, Lew Worsham, telling us our eyes should be focused "two inches behind the ball. This is the spot at which you should look." While the boys talk it over on the 19th, go out and try for yourself. Both techniques have worked for me.

Where should you try? I suggest the beach. When others are squandering their short time on this earth by wrinkling their skin in the sun, then cooling their bloodstream in the surf, sneak off to a lonely stretch of dunes with your wedge and a dozen balls. Slice at them for an hour or so. I did this one recent weekend on the sands of Bethany Beach in Delaware. Granted, I did receive a few strange glances at the time, but the admiring looks I later received back among the happy golfers in Washington were worth it. The first time I played after that practice in the dunes, I came out of the bunker five out of five times on the first try, three of them inside five feet. I've been flying as high as Saint-Exupéry since.

The Pleasures of the Short Hole

In conversations with golfers, I sometimes inquire about the roughest hole they've ever played. The answers tend to be similar. They talk about the giants: the 445 yard par four 5th on the Bethpage, Long Island, Black course; the 600 yard par five 9th at Congressional in Washington—the Ravine Hole—which no one has ever hit in two, not even Nicklaus who once tried with a dozen second shots. Or the 235 yard par three 16th at Cypress Point which few have hit in one. These are backbreaking holes that put us in traction, demanding booming rockets rather than crisp sparkling shots. They test strength, which is not the essence of golf, rather than finesse, which is.

On those occasions when someone asks for my nominee, I tell them about the 12th at The Moorings, a course in restful, undiscovered Vero Beach on Florida's east coast. The Mooring's 12th is a 275 yard par four. Doubtless, if the PGA ever held a tournament at this scenic course, this hole would be reduced to a par three. The 12th's difficulty is in its mental demands: an inlet of the Intercoastal Waterway runs the length of the hole on the left and a lagoon glistens 230 yards out on the right side. The green can be driven, but only by a precision blow that rolls through the narrow neck between the inlet and the lagoon. The mental demand is in choosing between the suggestions of imagination and memory: on the tee, do you imagine grandiosely that you can thread one through the neck or does the data bank of your memory remind you that you have dunked consecutive drives the last five times you have played the hole? The difficulty of the short, tight and well-designed golf hole is that the tiny room for error has so many windows and doors.

Many other holes at The Moorings are like that: short but bedeviling, forcing us to give up reliance on our muscle—as we should in golf—and exercise our mind. The problem here is that when playing one kind of hole many golfers think about another. They are wrestling the 445 yard monster they just played or are about to play—meanwhile they're too eager to take it easy on the lazy little hole that's a mere 275 yards.

We are too much conditioned by some of the less imaginative golf course architects. Supposedly "tough" courses usually play from 7,000 to 7,200 yards. This is a result of the macho influence in golf course design, an overreaction against the old slurs that a golfer's stamina is considerably less than, say, a downhill racer's. What a shame that when Jack Nicklaus built his course in Columbus, Ohio, he went for distance rather than finesse. The architects who create short but thought-provoking courses—like Pete Dye who designed The Moorings course as well as Harbour Town in South Carolina (named by many the toughest test on the tour) and John's Island, also in Vero—serve the game more faithfully than those who go for distance.

They can also serve the community. The Urban Land Institute gave over the January, 1976, issue of its magazine to discussing how "sensitive planning and common sense" can make the pastoral chemistry of the small golf course work for the community's good. The open spaces and greenery of a golf course can be the last defense against massive development. The ULI notes: "There is a list as long as one's imagination of multiple uses for acreage normally restricted to golf, thus providing a better cost-benefit ratio. Such a list includes bike trails, picnic areas, jogging courses, boating, lawn bowling, flower gardens and so on. The large courses, with their lavish clubhouses and overly manicured grounds, result in high costs and low utility. The shorter courses cost less to maintain but still provide the pleasure that people want from the game."

One of the earlier architects understanding the appeal of smallness was A. W. Tillinghast, who designed the west course at Winged Foot. He knew golf was not intended to torment the player and that exercising the mind to get a low score could in itself provide pleasure. An opportunity for such enjoyment is Winged Foot's 6th hole, a short tight 324 yard test.

In the several times I have played the hole, I never came to the tee without pausing and saying to myself, You're walking into a trap. Watch it, this hole isn't as simple as it looks. Because of the short yardage, the green looks as though it were just beyond the clipped grass of the tee.

Sometimes on the 6th, I have hit straight drives but then —easing up on the second shot—plunked it into the trap in front of the green or pumped it over the back into chaos. Other times, I have so tightened up on the tee that I pushed my drive into the right woods, not getting back to the fairway until several strokes and groans later. Once, (in 1956) when caddying for my brother Denis, during Winged

Foot's Anderson Memorial best-ball tournament, I saw a whole match turn around on the 6th. Denis and his partner drove into the woods on the right. Their opponents were in the middle, only 80 yards from the green. Denis's partner picked up after five futile tries at clearing the pines. Denis was luckier, though his second shot still left him about 100 yards behind his opponents' drives. The ball sat in a clover patch, so I counseled him to take less club as the ball would come out flying because of the oiliness of the clover. My advice was ignored, in the manner of older brothers knowing better than their juniors. As the ball sailed off and was in a flight that was obviously going to clear the green on a fly, I said, "You should have listened to me." Actually, what both of us next heard was the ball hitting the metal of a waterpipe covering in the far back of the apron around the green. Amazingly, the ball struck the rim of the covering and caromed back a foot from the pin. It was a sure par.

The opponents couldn't believe it. Unnerved, their once sure-thing 80 yard approach shots were now stern tests of delicacy. "Watch them blow it," I said to Denis. This time he listened. One opponent hit short and into the trap, the other hit long. Both took fives. That put them one down rather than the one up they thought they would be. They never recovered, partly because they seemed to be haunted throughout the round by the "clunk" sound when the ball hit the metal, but mostly I think because they were undone by losing such an "easy" hole.

The 6th at Winged Foot has been taking these kind of casualties for years. It illustrates, for still another time, that successful golf depends more on brain waves than on muscle striations. Players of awesome physical strength are easily defeated by the tiniest par four at Winged Foot. I can recall playing well up until the 6th—hitting the long 1st hole with a three iron second shot, getting close with a three wood on the 216 par three 3rd, home with a wedge on my third shot at the par five 5th. And then the wheels come flying off at the 6th.

During the 1974 U.S. Open at Winged Foot, I sometimes spent several hours stationed at the 6th to see how the best and the strongest did. Few passed through without trouble. According to figures from the IBM Sports Information Service, the 6th saw as many double bogies as the 2nd hole, even though the latter played almost 100 yards longer. The scoring average for the 6th during the tournament was 4.25, higher than the 382 yard 11th with 4.23. In the first and fourth rounds, competitors scored more birdies and pars on the long 435 14th than on the 6th.

The player who eventually won the tournament, Hale Irwin, is known on the tour as a thinking shotmaker. His two previous tour victories—up until then—had come at Harbour Town, which measures only 6,500 yards. At Winged Foot, Tillinghast must have relished designing those "easy" holes like the 6th. He once wrote that "a round of golf should represent 18 inspirations—not necessarily thrills, because spectacular holes may be sadly overdone. Every hole may be constructed to provide charm without being obtrusive with it. When I speak of a hole being inspiring, it is not intended to imply that the visitor is to be subject to attacks of hysteria on every teeing ground. It must be remembered that the great majority of golfers are aiming to reduce their previous performance by five strokes if possible, and if any one of them arrives at the home teeing ground with this possibility in reach, he is not caring too much whether he is driving off from a nearby ancient oak of majestic size, or from a dead sassafras. If his round ends happily, this is one beautiful course. . . ."

Tracking the Fugitive
Golf Ball

The statistical abstract of the Commerce Department doesn't list the number of golf balls lost annually, but we know that one hundred fifty-six million are manufactured every year. The golf professional wants to sell them to you, at $1.30 or $1.35 a piece, and this may be one reason you'll never get a lesson from him on how to find your lost Maxfli, Dot or Titleist. We get plenty of golf instruction on how to save strokes but not much on saving money.

A lost ball need not become a lost cause. Successful retrieval requires not so much good vision as basic attentiveness during the follow-through. When we snap a hook deep into the woods from the tee, most of us are either too shamed or enraged to note carefully its point of entry. But forget your pride or anger, unless you have posted forecaddies with compasses on either side of the fairway. As your hooking or slicing ball is entombing itself in a sylvan lostness, get a line on some tree, shrub or clump of grass where the ball was last seen. Those who learned the game by lugging other people's clubs know this as "marking," a habit that has nearly become an instinct with the alert caddy. With marking, the chances are greatly improved that the ball can be found. It assuredly isn't hiding from you because it resents the treatment you just gave it.

It is wise not only to watch when the ball careens into the woods but to listen also. When it went out of sight did you hear the melody of a xylophone—a little rhumba banged out on a couple of birches? Or did your shot penetrate clean? A careful recording of the sound effects could determine whether the melody ends on a sad or happy note.

The most aggravating lost ball is not the one deep in the forest—a little shade can be refreshing—but the one "right out in the open." This is the phrase golfers repeat as they roam around searching for a ball that lies just a few feet into the rough, that has trickled down the embankment behind the green, or has rolled into frog hair between two traps. "It has to be right here," they call out.

Right here again, attentiveness would have made a difference. Unfortunately, they saw only the general direction of the ball without noting the particulars. Ortega y Gasset said, "Tell me to what you pay attention and I will tell you what you are." If you're paying attention to the sun, sky and clouds when your ball is still moving 150 yards ahead, then you may be one of the hemisphere's finest naturalists, a fairway Thoreau, but you will soon be a frustrated duffer.

Even golfers who do have forecaddies are not assured of a flawless locator service. Gerald Ford was playing in a pro-amateur in Locust Grove, Virginia, when he sent his approach shot just slightly to right of a green. A *Washing-*

ton Post reporter was covering the scene, and what became newsworthy was not that Ford hit a wild one but that the Secret Service eagle-eyes couldn't find the ball. An estimated 30 agents searched in vain. Although some in the gallery were overheard muttering that the Secret Service was meant to protect the President against threats to his life, not protect him from mere two stroke penalties, the agents searched on. Meanwhile, the ball reposed in some long grass to the right of the green, not a hard place to find if someone had first taken a fix on the ball.

It is usually profitable to play late in the day, because at no other time are so many lost golf balls littering the course. You pick them up—in the short rough, just off the green, sometimes only a few yards from the tee—always wondering how anyone could have lost a ball there. Once I noticed a group of field crows—immense B-52 birds that need a runway to get aloft—congregating 50 yards ahead in some tall grass behind a fairway trap. I approached and discovered their fascination: three balls—shiny, the way crows like them—all within a yard of each other.

Until we stop losing our Titleists so needlessly in public, we will continue to draw the wrath not only of the players behind us (who want to play through) but occasionally also the poets. In despair, T.S. Eliot wrote in "The Rock:"

> And the wind shall say: 'Here were decent
> godless people:
> Their only monument the asphalt road
> And a thousand lost golf balls.'

We don't deserve to be remembered like that. Mark a fix. Listen to the trees. And watch the crows.

Commiseration

Golf demands an independent performance from us, in a way that few other sports do, yet it also asks us to be convivial. We may be alone in matching wits against the course but we usually do it in the companionship of others.

If companionship is one of the delights of golf, one of the necessities of being an amiable companion is practicing the art of commiseration. Such skills as sidehill putting or fading the ball around doglegs are nothing compared to knowing what to say, or saying nothing, when your partner scores straight sevens, leaves the ball in the trap four shots running or hits it fat into the lake. The averted gaze may get you past the first few scenes of ignominy, but in time—by the third hole, say—graciousness demands that you offer comment.

The comment should be sympathetic, not editorial, but what exactly are the choice words of commiseration? How hollow "tough luck" sounds as your partner's ball splashes mid-pond when both of you know that all the luck in the universe would not have carried him over the water. Can you sincerely say "nice try" when your opponent leaves a one foot putt three inches short of the cup, and he knows clearly it was actually a piteous try?

Some years ago, when I was qualifying for the U.S. Amateur, I received a well-deserved dressing down from one of those in my threesome. He was in the midst of a wretched round, his moods shifting from fury to despair and self-mockery. While his game was falling apart, he threw clubs, swore at his caddy and strung out a litany of blasphemy. Meanwhile, I was playing well. On the north course of the Montclair club in New Jersey, I was one under after six holes. Sunnily, I kept up a steady flow of commiseration: what a bad bounce, the wind took it, it would have made the green but for that limb. Finally, he could take no more of me. "Just keep quiet, will you," he cried out. I started to mumble an explanation, that I really was rooting for him, but I trailed off in mid-sentence. Commiseration was not what he needed, at least not the verbal kind.

The fates were merciless to my friend that day. Not even his blast at me brought his game around. But I had learned something, that on the golf course misery doesn't necessarily love company; it loves only relief, and if relief isn't forthcoming, then what misery loves next is silence. I kept mine for the remainder of the round, breaking it only at the end when my dejected friend handed me the scorecard. "You kept score well," I offered. He had no comment, except to stomp off morosely. But that hardly ruined my mood. I had qualified for the Amateur—played that year (1959) in Colorado Springs.

The problem of commiseration requires that we be alert

79 ·

to the sensibilities of disgrace. That may mean that we keep silent for a few holes. Deciding when to say nothing involves making a judgment on whether or not your partner's psyche can bear a comment—not immediately after a bad shot, but perhaps before the next one. If your partner has topped three consecutive shots, you might say as you walk the 10 yards to the next shot, "Keep the weight on the right side a little longer." If by magic, providence, or the law of averages, the next shot is well hit, your partner's spirit will not only be lifted from the slough of despond, but you will gain credit for astute observation.

Recently, I received credit in commiseration with a 16-handicapper. He had about a dozen things out of whack with his game. I didn't know which part of it to suggest he think about, because often this kind of golfer will indeed concentrate on one part of his swing, and let the rest slide. I decided to say nothing, to let him finish out the nine, drowning himself in a flash flood of double and triple bogies. He kept telling me how sorry he was to be holding me down (he was my partner in a high-and-low match), how he really played better, how he couldn't understand why he was falling apart. Walking off the ninth green, I had a hunch that the only commiseration he needed was a moment's rest from his agony. We went to the clubhouse, had a sandwich and talked about his law practice. It was flourishing, he said. A trial lawyer, he had just won an injury suit against an insurance company, collecting damages for his client over $200,000. He went on and on about the case. I listened as though nothing else mattered.

Going back to the 10th tee, I had the sense that he was a new man. I was hoping that he now saw himself as a skilled lawyer, not the drub who had just shot 53 on the front side. I was right. On the back nine, he came around. He shot a 40, with five pars and four bogies. The commiseration he needed from me was the passive kind—listening to his enthusiastic bragging about himself. It was a matter less of trying to remake his golf game than of remaking his self-image.

Sometimes, rather than offering a listening service, you may do immeasurable good by acknowledging the obvious. "That was a stupid shot" could be exactly what a player needs to hear after a stupid one. Hopefully, it will be understood that only a friend would speak so candidly, knowing frankness will not be mistaken for rudeness. Let politicians, tennis players and lovers hide their thoughts from each other, not golfers. By discreetly acknowledging the truth to a friend in agony you offer a passport to the world of pars and birdies from which your friend has been but temporarily exiled.

A Chip Off the Old Green

Mr. Chips was about to execute his favorite shot: 50 feet from the pin, six feet off the green in the manicured frog hair, with all of the heavens' solar energy warming the clubface of his five iron. The ball perched on a tuft of grass, Mr. Chips shifted his feet once, the way General George Washington would shift: confident and exact. He looked afresh at the pin, cast an eye on the break and stilled himself. His wrists cocked and the club drew back, slightly on the inside; the ball, off the back foot, was struck. It carried 15 feet in the air, bounced twice, skimmed a few feet and rolled to the break, veered right, skirted over the spike marks and dropped dead by the cup. "That's good," his opponent called out, moody and depressed, like General Howe conceding defeat at Yorktown.

This Mr. Chips is not the schoolmaster who taught Latin to the sixth form, but a younger relation who instead has mastered a more recent dead language: the eloquence of chip shots. He gets it up and down, as the unlettered say. He has to, because his short game is all he has that works. On the tee he resembles the greenskeeper scything July weeds. He hits no more than two or three greens in regulation, more often than not as a result of a fortunate bounce off a tree or ballwashing machine, and in sand traps he wanders like a thirsty traveler searching for an oasis.

Yet he stands at full height when, say, on a par four, his third lies on the apron 10 feet off the green. He may have arrived there after duck hooking a drive, skulling into the trap and bliffing out short; but now, on the apron, he is at his old stand. He knocks it stiff, gets his five and you, looking on amazed by the unfairness of life, golf and chip shot artists, three-putt from 15 feet to lose both the hole and your composure.

How does Mr. Chips do it? For a start, he selects the proper club—usually a five or six iron. Unless he has to carry a clump of weeds, come up over a hump or the ball has nestled low and needs to be dug out, why bother lofting the ball? Height is only one more problem to be solved. If the ball rests on the apron and the way is clear to the pin, no club is better than the five iron. All that needs to be thought out is the run. Such thinking isn't easy. At least you know a five iron will give you plenty of run, so a hard chop at the ball won't be necessary. Skilled chippers will check the surface of the green at the spot they'll be hitting to, tamping the green with the club head. If the green is soft, hit a little harder; if it's hard, hit soft.

After getting that straight, position the ball toward the back foot. This provides greater control, and will also help you hit the ball on the downswing. Too many golfers execute chip shots by scooping, as though the ball were an oyster in a pot of stew. Scoopers, who play the ball off the front foot (the ball is that much nearer the hole, they reason), lose control because their swing is longer. Reduce the room for error to a minimum on chip shots with a short swing.

Chipping requires a precise, tight swing, the hands low, the feet together and the body still. Especially a still body. Nothing should move in chipping except your hands and arms. Many golfers are poor chippers because they can't manage that stillness. They have all they can do to keep from moving when putting; consequently, motion off the green is a virtual craving.

Reliance on the five iron should be anything but rigid. When you have a close chip—just off the green but only a few feet of green to work with—use a nine iron. Bobby Locke, the knickered Englishman whom I saw play in 1953 at the old Palm Beach Round Robin at Meadowbrook, Long Island, chipped with a wedge. How odd it looked— that round man swinging roundly and sending the ball in a looping arc to the pin. When the ball ran close, as it often did, Locke would glance at the gallery with a wry smile.

Good chippers are scramblers, and off the course they usually live carefree lives, worrying as little as possible. They commit all the sins of golf and its extracurricular activities, save one: despair. They know that with one happy shot, disaster can be turned around.

Must Trouble Shots Be Troublesome?

"Nobody Knows the Trouble I've Seen" is an older tune than many realize. Where the song originated is anyone's guess. My own speculation is that it was a dirge first chanted by golfers lost in the woods and fog-rimmed marshes surrounding the legendary Scottish course St. Bogus.

And where is the present-day golfer who has not felt similar woes? Our ball behind a tree with six limbs between us and the fairway; our ball in front of a grass clump, a bunker in front of the green and a bunker to the left; or the green a pleasant 20 yards away with a slow-flowing brook at its edge. If a plea can be raised that in golf every shot is a trouble shot, then the defense will reply that some are more troubling than others.

After finding yourself in the rough, in a gulch, aiming toward a tiny crow's nest, and seeing it not as bad luck but as bad golf that got you there, three readily summoned guides can be recalled to get you out of trouble: "Calmness," "No Miracles" and "Head Down." Most golfers can focus on only one of these guides at a time, but that isn't enough. You must pay attention to all three.

"Calmness" requires you to develop basic self-consciousness, handy in a multitude of non-sporting pursuits. Trouble shots, more than any others, let us know who we are. Are we spineless or fearless? As Milton Berle, the noted 110-shooter of the Grossinger pro-ams, asked: "Man or mouse? Squeak up." To get into trouble, and then compound it by getting nervous, will not do you or your game much good. The golfers who refuse to calm themselves are easily identified. On finding themselves without a bridge over troubled waters, they curse, pace and stare. What have I done to be so ill-favored? Why have the gods turned away? But the message is clear: you've done something wrong, correct it. "Calmness" encourages you to look beyond the trouble and to learn what got you into the depths in the first place.

The second guide to lead you out of trouble speaks only two words: "No Miracles." You need only bring off a golf shot, not a miracle. From trouble, you simply need to get the ball back into play, not necessarily into the hole. Try that on the next shot, if you insist, when a failure won't get you into further trouble. Enjoyment in golf comes less reliably from the occasional miraculous shot than from the steady production of one good shot after another. Few who witnessed them can forget the glory days in the 1960s when Arnold Palmer was the boldest of the trouble shooters. Four or five times a round he would, like a fallen but vengeful angel, slash his way out of one layer of hell or another. Why settle for a routine birdie, he seemed to be thinking, when you can get a miracle par? I suspected for a long time, but never proved, that Mark McCormack, Palmer's money agent, used to tell his man to hit into the woods purposely. When Arnie fades it around six oaks to get on the green, the Army will whoop and yell, and hurry off to buy a new set of Palmer clubs. Into the 1970s, Palmer remains the best trouble shooter in golf; it's only the bedeviling fact that the rest of his game has faded.

Should the spirit stay calm and the ego controlled, the third guide, "Head Down," should still be heeded. No other shot causes the head to snap up so recklessly as the trouble shot. The common result is that the ball isn't hit, but topped. Or scraped. Don't be too eager to follow the ball, as though you can steer it through danger. The irony of the mis-hit trouble shot is that we look up to follow the ball only too well—a few dribbled yards ahead, into more trouble. As Sam Snead used to tell choppers he occasionally tortured himself by teaching: "You've just one problem. You stand too close to the ball—after you've hit it."

No golfer has ever played a round—some never a hole—without deservedly landing in a little trouble. And none has ever gotten out easily without the three guides: "Calmness," "No Miracles" and "Head Down." The three agree on one point: You get into trouble easily. Why not get out that way?

Are Love and Golf Compatible?

Happiness in love, statisticians keep telling us, has come upon hard times—connubial hardpan, golfers would call it. All the unloving couples of my acquaintance persist in one error: they do not play golf together. Perhaps somewhere a golfing couple does generate baleful loathing for each other, but I have never met a twosome whose shared delights on the fairways were not enough to cover the inevitable bad lies in the other parts of their lives.

First, the golfing couples who go on year after year defying the divorce statistics, and mystifying the neighbors who know well their obvious shortcomings, stay together, if for no other reason, because they suspect that perhaps no one else would tolerate their golf game. Second, golf is a means to companionship and, before the psychiatrists began selling us "growth" and "fulfillment," companionship was the reason long-lived couples went on forsaking all others. With golf in their lives, what else did they need?

Although non-golfing alliances of some years may be beyond hope, preventive action can be taken on others at the time we learn a couple is growing serious and thinking of marriage. Phone or go to them immediately. If one plays golf but the other doesn't, be candid and bold: assure them that the union will never work. The couple will laugh at you in proud protest, so thoroughly have they been deceived that love conquers all. It doesn't. It is defeated on lonely Saturdays and Sundays, and those interminably silent evenings when one is reading a golf magazine and the other has been reduced to solitaire for stimulation.

If golf, not eros, conquers all, let the conquest begin early in the relationship. Instead of wasting time lying about in bed on weekend mornings, the couple should get to the golf course early. Schopenhauer observed: "It is with trifles, and when he is off guard, that a man reveals his character," and the smart lover will note carefully how the beloved behaves on the fairways.

Golf creates lasting alliances because it provides couples with a fascinating topic of conversation, if only for one to tell the other, "You're away, dear." Often it's not much more than that. An article in *New York* magazine in 1973 told of a marriage counselor who wanted to know how much time married people spent talking to each other. He found a sampling of couples willing to subject themselves to the experiment and wired their homes and cars to record the syllables that passed their lips. The amount of time the couples spent talking to each other in a typical week averaged 27 minutes—or about 4 minutes per day. The couple who golf together are likely to talk that much just in discussing the wind conditions as they ascend the first tee. And from there, vistas of volubility lie ahead.

As for post-round exchanges, P. G. Wodehouse created

the definitive scene in his story, "Jane Gets Off the Fairway." Following their honeymoon playing "the well-known courses throughout the country," Jane and husband William "settled down to the normal life of a healthy young couple. Each day they did their round in the morning and their two rounds in the afternoon, and after dinner they would sit hand in hand in peaceful dusk, reminding one another of the best shots they had brought off at the various holes. Jane would describe to William how she got out of the bunker at the fifth, and William would describe to Jane the low, raking wind-cheater he did on the seventh, and then for a moment they would fall into the blissful silence which only true lovers know, until William, illustrating his remarks with a walking stick, would show Jane how he did that pin-splitter with the mashie on the sixteenth. An ideally happy union."

It may be too late to save relationships in which one golfs while the other gardens (or sulks). Some desperate couples do try to patch things by having the golfer teach the non-golfer how the game is played. But this can only lead to further justification for taking separate paths once the golfer learns in painful ways exactly how ungainly the other is where it really matters. In this case, nothing but applause should be given to the party that seeks a new playing partner. But care—high-quality care—should be taken by the suddenly freed golfer that the next mate have a palpable lust for the fairways. Has she the character to accept a string of sevens without throwing clubs or blaspheming? Is he forever talking about past feats while performing none in the present? Does he rake the bunkers (a good clue to whether he will wash the dishes after meals, or carry out the trash)? While being sized up, the lover should look to see if the beloved blames him for missed shots. Does he ask for a stroke a hole when he deserves only a half-stroke? There's a test for discovering the gold digger—ask her immediately after she sinks a putt for a birdie if she's willing to bear children right away so that in a few years the family will be a natural foursome.

If after similar practice rounds, you find your partner qualifying for the main event, go right ahead and get a blood test and a marriage license. It will be a long and smiling union.

The Purse You Lose May
Be Your Own:
Avoiding the Legal
Trials of Golf

Remember the prize-winning novel by J. F. Powers, *Morte
D'Urban*? That's the novel in which the 12th chapter begins: "Father Urban was taken unconscious to the hospital
in Great Plains where he was anointed by the chaplain,
x-rayed and heavily bandaged about the head by the doctors, and put to bed. He regained consciousness during the
night. By that time those who could have told him more of
what had happened had gone home. All he could find out
from the sisters was that he'd been struck in the head by
a golf ball."

Father Urban was konked as he approached the ninth
green, when another member of his foursome—a bishop,
no less—shot blind from over a hill. Theologically, Urban's
bang on the bean was what St. Teresa of Avila would have

called "an act of the loving God's will." But to be heretical for a moment, God had nothing to do with it. Urban should not have been walking ahead, much less when the wild-shooting bishop was hitting. Had Urban wanted to sue His Eminence—rather than merely complain to the Apostolic Delegate in Washington—he would not have had a prayer. He was in the wrong. Not only that, but he should have known—as any thinking golfer or any alert defense attorney would—that the golf course is a high-risk area where disaster can strike at any moment and where an awareness of safety may not save you strokes but may save your hide.

Few of us think of golf as dangerous but the list of its potential hazards to health is long. Death or injury can come by lightning, insect bite, sun stroke, heart attack, golf cart, stray shot, snake bite, falling tree limb or irate golfer. These forms of deadly golf say nothing of the endless ways you can do yourself in. In *The Golfer's Miscellany,* the classic work (from Harper & Row) by Percy Huggins, an entire chapter is devoted to "Fatal and Other Accidents on the Links." We are told of Edward M. Harrison who, while playing alone in 1951 at "the Inglewood Country Club, Seattle, apparently broke the shaft of his driver. The split shaft pierced his groin. He tried to reach the clubhouse, but collapsed and bled to death 100 yards from the 9th tee." In 1963, Harold Kalles of Toronto "died six days after his throat had been cut by a golf club shaft which broke against a tree as he was trying to play out of a bunker."

In 1956, "Myrl Hanmore died from an accident at the Riviera Country Club, Los Angeles, apparently caused when he lost control of a golf car on a steep incline and was crushed between the vehicle he was driving and one he was towing." In 1927, a Los Angeles man "was accidentally killed while giving his 12-year-old son a lesson. After showing the boy the correct way to drive, the father handed the club to him and stepped to one side. The boy attempted to follow his father's instructions but missed the ball, and the club caught his father on the right temple with considerable force, the man dying almost instantly." A final example—although the point has been made—involved a man at a Toronto course who "in October, 1966, holed his tee shot at the 8th green—and died from a heart attack on the 14th green."

These tales have a touch of morbid hilarity, because they seem to be flukes. Yet when lightning flashes, many golfers loft an umbrella and sit out in a golf cart, forgetting that both the umbrella and cart are conductors of electricity. If lightning threatens to strike, don't count on it to pass you by: avoid isolated trees, wire fences, hilltops and open spaces; get to shelter, the bigger the better. After that, don't worry about it. Lightning is not a major cause of death. According to a 1975 study by the U.S. Nuclear Regulatory Commission, lightning deaths per year total only 160. In fact, you have a far greater chance of being killed on the way to the golf course—for one in 4,000 die in motor vehicle crashes.

No statistics are available on the deaths due to stray shots from adjoining fairways. But the danger is ever present. When you hear "Fore!" three options are open. Do nothing, because you have heard the cry a thousand times before and never been hit. Look in the direction of the shot and try to see the ball coming at you. This was once my strategy until I missed being hit by inches. Two people had yelled, and I looked in the direction from which the ball *wasn't* coming. The last survival tactic is the best: when you hear "Fore!" duck and cover. Your companions will laugh at you, especially if the ball lands 50 yards away. But on rising take comfort that your health is intact, though perhaps not your dignity.

Flying golf balls are not the only worry. Clubs fly too. In September, 1975, a Montgomery County, Maryland, grand jury indicted a golfer on three counts of assault, including assault with intent to murder. According to police accounts, a foursome on the second tee of the Northwest Park public golf course wanted to play through a foursome down the fairway. When the foursome on the tee drove into the foursome ahead, one of the latter, angered, hit one of the balls from the trailing group into the woods. That brought the foursome from the tee charging down the fairway. A 15-minute fight broke out. Of the eight players, three were injured, and one was hospitalized with a skull fracture. Four golf clubs were broken in the melee. As of this writing, the case is pending.

Golfing your way into the courtroom may not always be as raw an experience as this, but the possibility of litigation—for or against you—is as much a part of golf as the slice. A few years ago, professional Sandra Haynie was playing in the Waterloo Open. Blasting out of a trap on one hole, her club hit an iron pipe buried in the sand. The unexpected jolt sent sharp pain through her neck and back, causing injuries. She sued the club's management and won a $4,250 judgment, a sum greater than if she had won the tournament.

What these court cases suggest is that before seeking an appointment with the golf pro to get your game in order, the canny golfer will consult an attorney or insurance agent—to learn the nature of the other kind of golfing trials that may lie ahead.

Ask your lawyer or insurance agent some questions like: am I liable for damages if my slice hits someone in another fairway because I didn't shout "Fore"? Or if I did shout "Fore" and this caused him to move into the line of flight? Can I sue the club manager or pro if I suffer bodily injury due to brake failure on the golf cart? Is my pro guilty of negligence when he tells me to lengthen my backswing and I do, but wrench my back and suffer a salary loss while I'm in traction in the hospital? Can I be tried for manslaughter if I three-putt from 12 feet, go into a tantrum and kill a playing partner when my violently thrown putter by chance crowns him in the head? Can I collect from Blue Cross if I take up golf to get out of a mental depression but find, after being unable to break 130, that my depression is worse and I need six months at Silver Hill?

The situations may seem unlikely, but so does much of reality before it happens. Consequently, the courts are filled with cases of golfers suing each other—by one estimate, made in 1966, 10,000 golfers are severly injured every year with bones broken, eyes blinded and domes concussed. You should not only take out comprehensive personal liability insurance, but understand the legal doctrine of "assumption of risk." This is what the time you spend on those 150 seemingly carefree acres of grass and trees represents to the legal-minded. It is also what a New Jersey court had in mind when it sided with a player whose shot hit another: "It is well known that not every shot played by a golfer goes to the point where he intended it should. If such were the case, every player would be perfect and the whole pleasure of the sport would be lost. It is common knowledge . . . that many bad shots must result, although every stroke is delivered with the best possible intention and without any negligence whatsoever." If the plaintiff was damned in that decision, he was blessed in another, in a Pennsylvania court: "It is the duty of every player to give timely warning and an adequate warning—usually by the word fore—of a shot which he is about to make and which he has reasonable grounds to believe may strike another player, caddy or spectator either on the same hole or a different hole."

What is illustrated by these decisions (both quoted from *Golf Digest,* June, 1964) is that no lawyer can tell for certain when you will or will not be held for damages when you tee off. The variables persist also in crashes involving golf carts. Since many cart manufacturers appear to care as little about safety as automobile manufacturers, if that can be imagined, it should be assumed that the brakes can give, the wheels fall out of place or the accelerator jam. Being a safe driver yourself is not enough, nor is avoiding the ride altogether. A case was recently reported from Florida in which "a country club rented a cart not equipped with the usual rubber brake pedal cover. The golfer who was renting it hit the brakes only to have his foot slip onto the accelerator so that he ran right into another golfer, who sued. The injured party was awarded damages from the club and the cart rental agency." For a few dollars a year, reputable insurance firms will cover you against golf cart crashes. The coverage is worth it; it was only a few years after carts were introduced that, in California alone, some 200 lawsuits involving carts were filed in a single year.

A final kind of useful insurance is the one sold by many clubs against holes-in-one. This will handle the bar bill, since the ace maker is expected to share his joy by buying everyone drinks. As a boy, I caddied once for an uninsured hole-in-one shooter at the Engineers Club, Roslyn, N.Y. Rather than pay for his luck, my man teed up a second ball, declaring the first ball—in the cup—unplayable. He scored a four on the second ball (five for the hole). He lost strokes but saved money. With insurance he could have saved both.

Playing it safe on the fairways means that, like most of this planet's pleasures, golf ought to be pursued by the cautious hedonist, not the giddy one. If Father Urban had known that, he might have risen to become a bishop rather than experience the spiritual conversion (from worldliness to belief) he underwent while convalescing from his head injury. Saying his breviary, preaching sermons, counseling the troubled—how much time can that leave for golf?

Long Shots Are Sure Shots

A few years ago, when I wanted to analyze how I might save three or four shots a round by better judgment of distances, I kept count of the number of times my shots into the green went past the cup. Usually, it was less than six times for 18 holes. Usually I was either short of the hole, if I made the green at all, or else I was short of the green altogether. The results are often the same among the touring pros. In the final round of the 1975 Masters, for example, Tom Weiskopf bogied the 16th hole because he underclubbed (with a five iron) and left himself short of the green; although an instinctive choker, Weiskopf had small chance of getting down in two for a par. In the same round Nicklaus bogied the 14th when his seven iron shot didn't reach the green. Both were topped by Tom Watson who took a quadruple bogey on the 16th after he dunked two consecutive shots in the pond in front of the green. Just as par proved impossible when someone hit short, it hardly made a difference when someone went long. Weiskopf carried over the 15th green but birdied it anyway.

Assuredly you'll do something wrong if you're too weak or too strong, but in golf, wrongs will be more easily righted if you risk hitting it over the green. To do this, no major adjustment in the swing is needed, only a measure of judiciousness in club selection. When it looks like an eight iron, take a seven. When you think a pond can be cleared with a four iron, hit a three, even a two.

A measure of humility is necessary to think long, because the imagination flourishes with the expectation of reaching the green with a five iron when other mortals need a three. We forget the last hole when we dumped our approach in the trap—a crisply hit shot, on line to the flag, but falling a yard short of clearing the sand. "It was heading straight to the pin" could be carved on the headstone of every golfer who died of grief because he never broke par. Of course we can announce to the world that our missed five iron, plopped now in the front trap, was directly on line. But how many listeners can we expect?

When I was a boy, the most perceptive caddy in the caddy yard where I learned the game was a fellow nicknamed "One More." He earned the best tips and was given the best loops because of his skills at what was called "clubbing." The members at the club were 100-shooters who had wasted their lives wresting fortunes from Wall Street and had lately joined the golf club to calm their nerves. Not a one knew anything about club selection— "Let's see, is it a four, seven, or nine iron," they would ask the caddy after sighting the green 140 yards away. "One More" had the gift of clubbing his player exactly right. When the latter would finally choose say, a six iron, he would be advised: "You need one more." The member would then hit a five and, more often than not, make it to the green, or at least near it. In the caddy yard, "One More" shared his secret with us groundlings. "I always tell them to take one more club than they think they need, and sometimes two more. I save those choppers about ten strokes a round. And I remind them of it at tipping time."

Too bad "One More" wasn't caddying for Arnold Palmer at the U.S. Open at Winged Foot in 1975. In the final round, Palmer was much in contention coming into the sixth hole, a 325 yard par four. Palmer, who rivals Weiskopf for finding ingenious ways to lose golf tournaments, played a wedge, but it wasn't enough club. The ball fell into the trap in front of the green. Palmer took a bogey and soon faded. Had "One More" been next to him to offer counsel, Palmer would have hit a nine iron, probably made the green and might have gone on to win. He was only seven over par at the time, but that score, however high it seemed then, turned out to be enough to win.

When selecting a club, it is crucial to remember that your mind is a flatterer: you're strong, you're bold, it whispers to your imagination. Think positive. Have confidence. With all those encouragements drifting inside your head, who is going to hit a seven or six iron when it's obvious that an eight is plenty. But the obvious is often illusory. Do something useful with your scorecard. Take along a notebook sometime and jot down how many times your approach shot gets past the hole. It will be all too few. Play the long shot, because it will usually prove out to be the sure shot.

Can Golf Be Child's Play?

It was going to be a big day. The father told his regular foursome he couldn't make it for the weekly game. After much pre-game buildup, he was taking his children to the course: a son 11 and a daughter 14.

The kids did what was asked. They came along. But rather than taking to the game, as their father had dreamed, they found the course a bore. The boy sulked and sneered for the 18 holes that his father played, his face brightening only when, behind the wheel of the golf cart (he demanded one), he tried to run a rabbit into a fence. The girl lasted three holes before expressing a desire to be someplace else—at her girlfriend's house getting a proper suntan by the side of the swimming pool. On the 10th hole, she was no longer talking because her pleas to quit at the end of nine had been ignored.

Similar scenes are not uncommon when parents attempt to get their sons and daughters "interested" in golf; their mistakes are often similar: they talk up the game too much, or they make it a required course. What child wouldn't rebel or want to be somewhere else when a tour around the front nine is less a walk in the sun than a forced march.

So much for the problem. The solution is simple: children cannot be taught golf, they can only be exposed to it. Do that naturally and they will learn the game themselves: as they learn the far more difficult skills of walking and talking. Compared to those feats, golf is easy.

I remember this from my own boyhood: with never a word to me about the pleasures of golf, my father let the golf bug bite me by means of tender nips over a period of years. I was eight when I noticed his golf clubs hanging on a hook in the garage. I took them out and tried hitting a baseball with them. That didn't work, so I then went for the pine cones among the trees along the lawn. For the rest of that summer, I hit nothing but pine cones. My father noted this but discreetly said nothing about what he would have called "the better suitability" of golf balls. In fact, he would often hit the pine cones with me, both of us enjoying it immensely. The next summer, he left some golf balls on the lawn. I tried hitting them. They went further than the pine cones, so I stuck with them.

One afternoon the next summer, I noticed a man digging holes in the lawn. We lived in Old Brookville on the north shore of Long Island, with an acre of mowed grass around our home, and my father had asked the greenskeeper from his golf club (the Brookville Country Club, where he was the first club champion) to come over, put in four of those holes, and stick little red flags in them. With the 100-odd shag balls my father used to practice chipping, I began aiming for the flags. During the next two summers, I must have hit thousands of shots. When pals from school came over, we held our own tournaments on the four hole course. When I was 12, I asked my father if I could go with him and my older brothers when they went to play a few holes in the evening at Brookville. "If you'd like to come," he said, "we'd like to have you."

I don't think any father has ever introduced his children to golf more wisely or more gently than that. No pushing, no sermonizing, no cajoling. He merely laid out a few minor temptations for the imagination, knowing a child's natural curiosity would do the rest.

I am doing this now with my own children. I have left my golf clubs and golf balls around the house. They have picked them up, taken them outside (after minor damage to a hallway mirror) and tried to figure out exactly how to use them. One evening, when I was going out to play a few holes in the evening, my eight-year-old asked if he could come along. When the seven-year-old and four-year-old saw us leaving they wanted in, too. So we were a foursome, then a fivesome, because my wife wanted to play too. That evening, we went only three holes. The boys tried hitting only a few shots. The rest of the time, they mostly ran through the sand traps, climbed trees and raced downhill, laughing and singing with the wind.

That's all they've done those few other times we've all gone out to the golf course. But I think I've made a good beginning. In their minds, a golf course is a place for fun. It makes little difference if, for now, they are getting a different kind of pleasure from the golf course than I am. I don't care to climb trees or make dust storms in the bunkers. But what I do—hitting the ball up and down the hills, over the trees and out of the sand—must surely strike the boys as a strange way to take advantage of the immense funny-shaped lawn that's a golf course.

I have noticed that increasingly the boys want to hit shots. The closer we are to the hole, the greater their desire. My four-year-old would prefer to do nothing but stay on the green—which some evenings is all that we do. We devise contests, such as the three of them standing astride in front of the hole, seeing if I can putt the ball under them from 50 feet away. Or I take the straddle position and let them try.

I have been cautious about handing out advice. One of the boys spent a summer hitting cross-handed; the next summer, on his own, he tried it the right way. It felt better and he stuck with it. I have seen parents make an issue out of an improper grip, only to kill the child's enthusiasm because the supposedly right way felt strange and uncomfortable.

I haven't made up my mind about letting children compete in junior tournaments. Stories are told of Johnny Miller, age nine, confined to the back yard, hitting bucket after bucket of golf balls into a net—all to get him ready for a peewee tournament his father wanted him to win. Children don't need to know about winning or losing until they're much older. Let them discover competition on their own, which they will when they will be emotionally ready for it.

The first tournament I played in was a caddy's day "championship," an event organized at the end of the summer at the Engineer's Club in Roslyn, N.Y. (where Chick Evans defeated Francis Oiumet 7 and 6 in the 1920 U.S. Amateur). I shot 124. The score didn't matter to me as much as the idea that I could play in the tournament at all. The boy who did win—with a 78—developed an enormous ego in the caddy yard. And that was about all that developed in him. His golf game, over the summers, never much improved. He had peaked too early. Meanwhile, during three summers in the Engineers Open, my score went from 124 to 96 to 81. I played so well at the age of 16 that some of my fellow caddies said I was better than the pro. The latter was a fellow named Jack Oliver, whose considerable pride was offended by the talk in the caddy yard, so he accepted a challenge from me, provided my backers and I could come up with a $50 bet. That was heavy action, in 1954 dollars. The match—stroke play—created a small stir at the club. When we teed off—on a Monday when the members were absent—Oliver was confident I wouldn't even complete the round. But, with nearly one hundred caddies in the gallery, I made out all right. I shot a 74 to his 80. My backers won their $50, but I earned nothing. Oliver gave me a press bet on the last hole. I was too green to admit I didn't know that a press bet was a bet on just that hole, so I said sure. I was seven strokes ahead on the original bet, so I eased up on the last hole, making a safe conservative bogey five to Oliver's par four.

The match was a hard introduction into the economics of golf, but it confirmed that the early exposure my father had given me was sound. "Where'd you learn to chip like that," Oliver asked after the round. I had hit only five greens on the long, hilly Engineers course, but got up and down on 11 of the 13 greens that I missed. "Hitting pine combs," I said. He thought I was giving him lip.

Coping with the Critics of Golf

When Calvin Coolidge dumped on golfers by declaiming that he "did not see the sense in chasing a little white ball around a field," he was among the first of what is now a legion of critics who think golfers are stupid, immoral or beyond salvation. Over the years, we have been easy targets for many a cheap shot.

My own stomach has been especially ulcerated by the words of Mother Jones, the great assailer of management who recounted in her autobiography a speech she gave in 1902 to the striking coal miners of West Virginia: "Good-bye boys. I'm under arrest. I may have to go to jail. I may not see you for a long time. Keep up this fight. Don't surrender. Pay no attention to the injunction machine at Parkersburg. The federal judge is a scab anyhow. While you starve, he plays golf."

A poem entitled "Golfers" by John Updike in a 1975 issue of *The New Republic* at least equalled the sharpness of Mother Jones:

One-gloved beasts in cleats, they come clattering
down to the locker room in bogus triumph, bulls
with the pics of their pars still noisy in them,
breathing false fire of stride, strike, strike, and putt.
We dread them, their brown arms and rasp of money,
their slacks the color of ice cream, their shoes whiter
than bones that stipple the downtrodden green,
that take an open stance on the backs of the poor.

What is it about golf and its addicts that arouses this hostility? One theory is that because golf is seen as a rich man's sport anyone who plays it deserves all the loathing the world can give him.

One trouble with this theory is that not an excessive number of the rich really do play golf. According to the figures of the National Golf Foundation, out of the 11,370 golf courses in the United States, only 5,897 are privately owned and restricted to members only. The other 5,473 are open to public play. The figures are not surprising. The wealthy can't afford the time it takes to complete a round of golf. Even on the fairways, they are often preoccupied with phoning the office. When you notice phone booths installed at strategic points between fairways, you can be sure you are playing not far from the rich. After taking a nine on the hole, they sense it's time to call Miss Tidgewell to see how the market is doing.

Preoccupation with business was the downfall of Arnold Palmer. He became a millionaire from his golf earnings but then became so intent on getting more bucks from his marketability that he let go of his golf game. He has yet to regain it (he can't concentrate, he says), and has not won a major tournament since 1964. In 1975, he was reduced to the ignominy of going abroad to win such minor events as the Spanish Open and the British PGA.

Strong evidence that golf is not a sport reserved for the rich has been offered by the Attorney General of Maryland. In early 1976, sensing a safe political issue, he sent to a number of Maryland country clubs a five page, 32-item questionnaire trying to learn which clubs discriminated on the basis of sex, race or religion. When the answers came back, 16 of the clubs were notified by the Attorney General that "based on your response to the questionnaire, this office has determined that it will be necessary to hold a public hearing on the issue of whether (the) club is in compliance" with the law. This lawman can afford to be bold in pursuing rich golfers because it is the thousandaires of the community who help support the clubs. Because of preferential tax assessments clubs in the suburban Washington areas of Montgomery and Prince George's counties were allowed write-offs in 1975 totaling $638,000. For the Chevy Chase Club, the sum was $88,000, and Burning Tree wrote off $50,000. Before the state legislature changed the laws, the justification for the tax breaks was that country clubs were "open spaces" worth preserving for the community's own good. The greenery is good for you, was the idea, even if the club is fenced in by barbed wire to keep the public from getting at it.

Golfers are vulnerable to such charges, but the law is at work to correct the abuses. Where the law may not be working so fast is to correct the sexism that many clubs allow. It is common for "the ladies" to be restricted to certain starting times, presumably past one or two o'clock on the weekends and perhaps Wednesdays. The idea is to keep the slower moving women off the parade grounds so the faster paced men can march around without interference. This might make sense if it could be proven that men are faster players than women. Since that is not the case, restricted starting times should be assigned according to talent, not sex. Let the high-scoring and presumably slower players onto the course after, say 2 P.M., without sexual consideration.

Course managements don't see it that way. And this vision isn't likely to change until women, and male sympathizers, begin pressuring for clubs to change. A precedent does exist. Decades ago, a group of Long Island women kicked up so many divots about restrictions against them that their husbands built them a club of their own: The Women's National Golf Club in Glen Head, Long Island. It became a model of woman power for a number of years. But in time the real estate taxes became too much and the land was sold to a group who established a Jewish country club.

However, women's golf clubs aren't the answer. That serves only to increase segregation. Instead, clubs are needed where the sole qualification for membership is an enthusiasm for golf and the means to pay for the pleasures. Such a qualification would remove a few bricks from the racial and religious walls that are now built symbolically around golf courses and which bring onto the game much of the criticism it deserves.

More than a few country clubs now hard-up for money are conducting membership drives free of the old biases. Anyone can get in, a fact that prompted Groucho Marx to make the wry comment that he didn't want to join a certain Los Angeles golf club because any organization which would have him for a member wasn't worth joining. Ironically, many of the public courses are so well run and kept up that citizens find their golf urges well satisfied by the daily greens fee system. Why become a member of a country club when you are already a member of the human race? As it is, many private clubs are as crowded as the public ones, as public course players can gleefully note as they drive past the "members only" clubs and see the holes clogged and backed up.

The critics of golf are often the very ones with whom we

live, putting aside Calvin Coolidge, Mother Jones and the rest. A friend of mine has been catching it for years from his wife. He plays once on the weekends, once during the week. He is called a "golf nut" by his wife, a harsh description because golf nuttiness doesn't begin, at least by my measurements, until a person plays at least 27 holes a day. Another friend, a married woman in her early 50s, takes heat from her husband because she dares spend Tuesdays at the golf course. She has a regular foursome. What rankles the old man is that the women's game consumes more than five hours' play. That means he has to cook supper for himself. The dear woman escapes the kitchen for one day a week and the husband is low enough to criticize her for playing golf leisurely enough to enjoy the game.

The only complaint that non-golfers should justifiably have against us is that providence has singled us out for pleasures denied to other mortals. Indeed, the highest pleasure of golf may be that on the fairways and far from all the pressures of commerce and rationality, we can feel immortal for a few hours.

The Ethics of Onlooking

The PGA tour, beginning in January and tapering off in November, involves about 300 players competing in some 45 tournaments for a total of about $8 million in prize money. I played in some of the PGA tournaments while in college in the late 1950s, and since then I have been a spectator as often as possible. I have seen some fine players execute memorable shots, but I remember no tournament more vividly than the 1972 Westchester Golf Classic, the richest mother lode on the tour that year. My memories are not of the winner but of one of the losers, and my own involvement in his loss. What happened is worth recounting because it acknowledges that being a spectator can sometimes take us far beyond mere onlooking.

I went to Westchester to watch Chuck Thorpe. Known

for his power off the tee, Thorpe had occasionally demonstrated the power of his tongue, talking big about himself,
a little like Muhammad Ali. Some of the tour veterans
didn't like Thorpe's bragging, for he was a rookie—and a
black one at that.

I knew about Thorpe because he had played in the
Washington area for a while, before he qualified for the
tour at the PGA school in Florida. I planned on writing
something about him based on what I might see at Westchester. He had played well a few weeks before in the PGA
championship, and among the black players on the tour
he, as much as any, had a chance to do well.

I didn't catch up to Thorpe at Westchester until the 15th
hole of the second round. By the end of the day, however,
a series of unlikely events had drawn both of us into a
drama involving the ethics of his profession and mine.
Thorpe was to be disqualified from play and I was to have
a story far different from the one I planned. Each of us,
however, met standards anyone should expect from others
in a like situation.

When I found Thorpe, he had only four holes left to play.
He bogied 15 and 16 as a result of sloppy shotmaking and
was one over par, a score that would be close to the cutoff
for the final 36 holes. On 17, an easy and short par four,
Thorpe, tense or lazy, flubbed his second shot to the green.
His third, a wedge, hit the green—about 30 feet away from
the cup. His playing partners, Dick Crawford and Roy
Pace, were closer to the cup, so Thorpe putted first, strok-
ing it close, no more than a foot away. Then, hesitating—
he was in Pace's line and not sure whether to putt out or
mark his ball—Thorpe jabbed at his one-footer, and
missed. His score was six, and the others putted out for
their pars.

On the 18th, a par five, Thorpe got hold of himself and
drilled a two iron to the green about 12 feet from the hole
and two-putted for a birdie. The gallery that trailed him

—I was about 20 percent of it—cheered at the home green because the birdie brought him in at 146: a 72 on Thursday and 74 on Friday. It was a score, from a look at the leaderboard, that might make the cut. Following the round, I interviewed the tall and muscular player. We stood near the press tent away from the milling crowds. Thorpe was soft-spoken, a likeable young man. He told of his being one of 13 children from a small North Carolina town and of learning golf by playing on caddy's day at a white country club where his father tended greens.

An hour later, after Thorpe had gone his way, I happened to look at the official scoreboard off the 18th fairway. Thorpe's score was posted as 145, with a five on the 17th, not the six I had seen him take. I waited another hour to see if the correction would be made, but the five stood. Whatever the cause, a rule had been broken. The PGA requires each player to keep the score of a playing partner; at the end of the round the players check their scorecards hole by hole for accuracy. Mistakes are occasionally made—the DiVicenzo case at the Masters in 1968 when he signed an incorrect scorecard, is well known—and disqualification is the automatic penalty even when a higher score is unintentionally substituted for a higher one.

With unwelcomed suddenness, I faced the painful fact that no one else had noticed the error and that Thorpe's fate at Westchester was at the mercy of my judgment: to be silent about the rule infraction or go to a PGA official to report it. If Thorpe's score was 150 or 153, it would have made no difference—he would have been out anyway. But his 145 as posted appeared likely to be the cutoff, and by day's end, it was. Arnold Palmer, the defending champion, with a 146, packed off in dejection.

I had gone to the tournament as part of my vacation, with no intention of getting involved in a conflict. But how do you hide? To be silent meant Thorpe would play the final 36 holes, be guaranteed a few hundred dollars at least and perhaps—if he played well—thousands. He would also be exempt from the ordeal of Monday qualifying at the next tournament. Looking the other way also meant boosting my fan sympathies for Thorpe, a rookie athlete in a lonely and competitive sport, a self-taught player who'd had few of the breaks of the average tour player who learns the game at a country club and perfects it in college. Even the foolish way Thorpe missed the one-footer at 17 earned him my sympathy: it was the kind of mistake pros make early in their amateur days and junior tournaments. The experienced and careful golfer, knowing a tap-in putt equals a 300-yard drive on the scorecard, does not rush his pace to get out of another player's line, as Thorpe had done. Instead, the experienced pro marks the ball and holes out later—in full concentration. This is a lesson the fair-haired Millers and Nicklauses learned at their leisure as touring youngsters, but which Thorpe, denied entrance to early doors, was learning on the job.

Before deciding to tell the PGA officials about the 17th hole score, I tried to find Thorpe. I couldn't. He was neither at the club nor his hotel. I found Crawford, though, who had kept Thorpe's scorecard. By a fluke, Crawford was also involved in a dispute. He had been penalized two strokes for being late on the first tee; his clubs had been stolen from the locker room, and in hunting around for a new set he had shown up late for his starting time. Crawford, distracted all afternoon by the PGA's dogmatic penalty—why couldn't they have made an exception for this lateness when the reason was clearly justified?—said he wasn't watching Thorpe on 17 and put down a five believing Thorpe had made the "gimmie." In the scorer's tent following play, Thorpe, surely downcast by his play and perhaps distracted by Crawford's being victimized by both a thief and the PGA (Crawford missed the cut by two strokes, the same two he was penalized), may not have noticed his inaccurate scorecard.

With the intention of correcting an oversight (the missing missed putt) and not exposing cheating—I don't believe Thorpe had been trying to pull a fast one in any way —I went to a PGA official in the late afternoon. The third member of the threesome, Roy Pace, an unknown Texas pro who had played well at Westchester, was present and confirmed Thorpe's six. I had spent about an hour trying to find Pace because I wanted to let him know what I knew and get his side of the story.

A few hours later, the PGA located Thorpe. I wasn't on hand for the conversation but, apparently, he confirmed that his score on 17 really was six, not five. Thorpe was disqualified from the tournament.

If only Thorpe had made that tap-in putt—for his profit and my relaxation. I don't know if the PGA told him or anyone else about my involvement. Probably not. At first, the officials with whom I spoke seemed annoyed by the information I brought them. But they realized, after a few moments' reflection, that they had better act on what I'd told them, if only to avoid anything I might write about the incident. An article could easily raise questions about the PGA if it were reported that they had done nothing to rectify an incorrect score.

Thorpe played in a few more tournaments that year, but since then has dropped from sight. I notice his name occasionally in some of the regional tournaments sponsored by the Middle Atlantic PGA, but he is off the tour itself. My hope after Westchester was that he go on to a rewarding career in the game. I thought that it was perhaps better that he had committed those errors—hasty putting and careless score-checking—at Westchester than later on, say in the U.S. Open or the PGA. I thought he had the talent to win both. It's likely that he still does. Should he one day win a championship, I will be one of those pleased to recall that I knew Thorpe when he was on the way up. And to recall that I didn't mar his rise by a "helpful" look the other way.

Cutting Short the Backswing

While trying my one-footers on the practice green recently, a companion suggested I look over to the nearby
first tee. The young man about to drive had been tabbed by
the local pro as a rising star. I looked at tomorrow's Johnny
Miller and the 16-year-old husky did indeed have the aura
of a champ: his golf bag weighed 75 pounds (not including
his pom-pom head covers), his driver had the fabled
graphite shaft and silver ball markers jingled in his
pocket. "I'm impressed," I said. The prodigy, after 15 or 20
seconds of pre-swing concentration that someone had put
into his head as a necessity for good golf, finally swung.

The spectacle was amazing. The boy brought his hands
so high up on the backswing that the club, had it had a
whippy shaft, would have wrapped around his neck. As it

was, the backswing was extended so far that, at the top, the clubhead could be easily seen out of his left eye. I found it astonishing that he could execute a downswing at all and still get to the ball. "Whatever trophies and cups you have won to date," I wanted to call out, "keep shining them, lad. With a swing like that, they may be your last."

The flaw in the youngster's excessive swing was its uselessness. Overswinging is so common an ailment among golfers that many have all but forgotten the practicality of the short swing. What is accomplished by taking the club so far back and around that instead of swinging, you are turning like a corkscrew? The craving for extra distance is one motivation for the mega-swing. But economy of exertion on the backswing doesn't mean that potential energy is lost, simply that it is compacted. The energy is still present, and with a short swing—still keeping an arc—you use only the amount you need. Overswinging golfers want to hit a long ball and think they must tee off with the long swing. But believe me, you strike the ball cleaner, hit it as far and feel as happy with a short swing as with a long one.

To develop a short swing, you must understand that the hitting area is reached when the downswinging hands are at the level of right hip, not when they start down from the shoulders. The shaft of the club—if a still action camera were used—would be seen as being vertical to the ground at this moment. This is the point in the arc of the swing when the power should be turned on. Not much else is going to matter, especially not how grandly you have flailed your hands and the club on the backswing. That extracurricular motion can only alter your timing and increase the room you have to botch it with the hips, shoulders and rear end getting into the act.

To develop a short swing, try hitting the ball with one hand. I have played whole rounds this way, most recently when I could get no other bet from a friend, except to take him on one-handed. He wanted to play conventional golf, so the bet involved my playing one ball with one hand and his playing two with two hands: my total score with one ball against his total with two. It was no match. I shot a 98 and he a 153 (a 78 on one ball and 75 on the other). For the rematch, he suggested I hit with one hand while standing on one foot. I declined. I had already gotten what I wanted: a better and shorter swing. A one-handed round a few times a year assures that your two-handed swing will improve. You don't take the club back as far, and the hitting area receives the power from your arm in concentrated form. In addition, if you do swing too long, it feels strange, because that's how it felt when you were swinging one-handed if you went back too far.

At the moment, the tour has a number of players—Crenshaw and Wadkins, among others—who overswing, so it's not a surprise that so many high school and college golfers pattern their swings after these youthful stars.

Among the seasoned pros, Lee Trevino has a model short swing. My boyhood hero, Tommy Bolt, had one, and a few years ago Doug Sanders had what may have been the best short swing of all.

My own swing is as short as I can make it. Aside from better control of the ball, the other advantage I have is that after a long layoff, I need only a round or two to get my game back. In the spring, after a golfless winter, I can get into the 70s with little trouble, while my partners with long backswings need weeks—some of them until mid-summer—to play well. It's a strain to watch them. They are like giant farm machines being hauled out of winter storage. The gears are oiled, the axles are greased, the wheels are adjusted, the engine cleaned and then the whole contraption moves a few yards before the fan belt snaps. Like the overswinging golfer, the machine does well when it works, but getting it to work at all is the wonder.

Calling the Shots

Predicting the outcome of golf tournaments can be one of the game's modest pleasures. I have been doing it since 1958 when, in the company of friends after a round of golf, I correctly forecast that Tommy Bolt would win the U.S. Open, with Julius Boros and Gary Player behind him. Of course, I had picked Tommy Bolt to win every Open in which he played, since he went on the tour in the early 1950 so my accuracy in 1958 may not have been that amazing. Regardless of the outcome, however, getting together with a few companions to "call the shots" is a pleasure not to be missed.

The major championships are best for predictions. A method that offers breadth, and forces you to reflect is one in which you list six players you think will win and six you think won't win. Write down your reasons, keep a copy for yourself and send one to a friend. And ask for your friend's predictions. After the tournament, both of you can enjoy a few hours of discussion that has some flavor, rather than aimless talk about the tournament, because you will be talking about your own involvement in the competition. You were watching the tournament but the watching—because of your forecasts—was active, not passive. You had a stake.

Predicting winners is not easy. At the invitation of George Solomon, the sports editor of *The Washington Post,* I went into print with forecasts for the 1976 Open and the 1976 PGA. It is hazardous duty, because newspaper readers enjoy nothing more than catching "the experts" in open wrongheadedness. Journalists are as blundering as anyone, except that we are generally highly skilled at covering it over, if not up. So when a writer comes along and risks making mistakes in public view, the hazards are taken on knowingly. Being an editorial writer at the *Post* for 10 years, I saw no reason not to bring a few opinions also to the sports pages.

In picking losers, I had a perfect record for both tournaments. For both the Open and the PGA, I said that neither Nicklaus, Weiskopf or Palmer would win. They didn't. I enjoyed making these forecasts because these three divine ones are inevitably picked as favorites for every major championship, year after year. I also picked Johnny Miller to lose in the Open—which was accurate—and would have stuck with that forecast for the PGA had he not withdrawn two days before.

I don't know how many of the pros playing in the Open —held in Atlanta in 1976—paid attention to my picks. Not many, I suspect, because who among them would read the *Post,* an out-of-town newspaper? But it was a different matter when the PGA was held at Congressional, a few miles outside of Washington, and the *Post* sports pages were what the players read over breakfast. These were my picks for probable losers along with my reasons:

Tom Weiskopf—At the British Open in July, when telling the press what a sensitive soul he was, Weiskopf said, "I have a great talent."

It's good he thinks so, because based on his record no one else does. But let's be easy on Talented Tom, or he'll stomp off Congressional in another of his regular pouts. To keep him around, the PGA should let him play from the white markers. But he still couldn't win, because he is only an average putter.

Arnold Palmer—He'll be ready for the PGA seniors soon, where against geriatrics like Ed Furgol, Ernie Catropa and Gene Sarazen, victories will be easy. His last "success" was the 1975 La Manga Open in Spain. Golf is a torment for Palmer these days. The Army still comes out but they are more often an irritation for him—wildly cheering weak drives or poor approaches. When they shout out "Remember Cherry Hills" it only reminds Palmer that his day is long past. He threw away his talent to run his businesses.

Lee Elder—He played a practice round at Congressional with Gerald Ford two weeks ago and outdrove the President on the first hole only by 10 yards. With his short drives, Elder will be worn down by hitting woods and long irons into the par fours. Unless the snakes are dropping on the greens, he'll be happy to make the cut.

Jack Nicklaus—Jack the Businessman has let his game go, in favor of real estate deals (his Muirfield operation), hustling shirts, cars and express cards. He'll be straining to win here, to prove that he hasn't lost it, but Congressional has strains of its own that are enough to defeat Nicklaus.

Hale Irwin—He's yet to get over losing to Roger Maltbie at Muirfield. Irwin's trouble is that he has let himself be-

lieve all the press accounts that he is a new superstar and a threat every time he merely tees up. Actually, his only major win, at Winged Foot in '74, came when others in the field caved in and he just happened to be lucky in hanging on.

For possible winners, I wrote:

Ben Crenshaw—He's the best putter to come along since Billy Casper. To date, he's been content to be just "Gentle Ben" but he is learning fast to muster some sustained intensity and overcome the "big bogey" tendency on the final nine holes. He needs also to shorten his swing a little. But he's talented, has instinct and can play long courses.

Al Geiberger—This is the Year of the Peanut,* so why not for Skippy Geiberger? Actually, he's about as colorless as those sandwiches he's said to thrive on, but he plays steady golf, keeps it straight and doesn't take himself seriously. Good qualities.

Tom Watson—He's won at Butler, the toughest long course on the tour. He has self-confidence and isn't put off when he takes a couple of bogies. He is good at playing himself back into contention, after a few painful experiences (Winged Foot in '74) at blowing leads.

Ray Floyd—He played well here in the 1964 Open when he was overshadowed by his final-day pairing with Venturi. He's lost his baby-fat since then and has also mastered the five wood. It's a good club for Congressional.

Lee Trevino—Will the layoff help him? He has enough natural talent, not to mention verve, to carry him over 10 years of inaction, not just a month or so. Congressional's greens will be on the slow side, and Trevino can handle them. He's also the tour's straightest driver.

Bob Murphy—I know. In June, I picked him to win the Open and he didn't even survive the cut. I paid for it. The

---

*I was right, at least, in picking Jimmy Carter.

Post ran a stinging letter-to-the-editor about my stupid-
ity. But I'm with Murph whenever he plays. I still weep
over that six he had on the 72nd hole at Medinah. Murphy
is too fat, too easygoing and too Irish, but on the tour—
among all those grim and solemn ones—he's a delight.
Pull yourself together, Murph, and don't humiliate me
again!

I thought I did well with these forecasts, considering
that none of my losers won and one of my winners—Ray
Floyd—finished but a stroke behind the man who did win,
Dave Stockton. In addition, Crenshaw and Watson
finished in the top ten.

The reaction to my printed forecasts couldn't be mea-
sured on the day they appeared—the Wednesday before
the tournament. But I was told that my column was the
buzz of the locker room and the press tent. Indeed, what
kind of wild man was this McCarthy to say such Golden
Boys as Nicklaus and Weiskopf wouldn't win, when they
were the favorites of everyone else?

It was with some apparent delight that after Weiskopf
led the first round of the PGA with a 65 he held forth in the
post-round press conference about my column. Talented
Tom was testy: "Some of it was humorous, some of it was
pretty strong. Controversy is part of a major championship. Maybe he writes like that all the time . . . I don't
know." *The Miami Herald* headline read: "Weiskopf
Shrugs Off Taunts for One Stroke Lead in the PGA." It ran
over an AP story saying that Weiskopf was "angered by the
printed taunts of a Washington newspaper columnist."
Tom was going to rub my nose in it, watch out. *The Wash-*
ington Star, eager to do the job for him, dismissed my
column as "a rather silly piece—some harmless sensation-
alism."

For a moment or two—but no more—it looked bad for
me. But I had little doubt that Weiskopf, no matter that he

shot an opening 65, would find a way to lose. The next day, with a 74, his explorations began and he was out of it with another poor round on Saturday. I was reminded of what I said of him in the Open: he "knows more ways of choking than Dracula."

Much of the mail that followed my Open and PGA columns gleefully swung at the chin I had exposed for punching. I hadn't picked a winner either time, and readers want perfection. It didn't matter that others were going with safe picks. A *Washington Star* writer said the winner should emerge from Crenshaw, Geiberger, Green, Hayes, Irwin, Nicklaus, Pate, Snead, Watson and Weiskopf. That was fearless, those being the ten leading money winners. The *Star* hadn't learned anything from the year before when one of its sportswriters said of the Open (held at Medinah in Chicago) that "this tournament is the property of the superstars. People like Jack Nicklaus, Lee Trevino, Tom Weiskopf, Gary Player, Johnny Miller and Hale Irwin." As for the lesser lights of the tour, it was said that by the end of the tournament "they will be gone." They weren't gone, as we know. The winner was not one of the sure-shot superstars but a longshot, Lou Graham. At Congressional in 1976, even with one round to go, no one was accurately picking the winner. With most of the field out of it, Dave Marr wrote in *The Washington Star* that Nicklaus, two shots behind, would probably take it. Five others —all within easy striking distance—also had good chances, so good in fact that he wrote, "that leaves out such prominent players as Dave Stockton . . ."

Forecasting is difficult because it is all but impossible to assess the state of mind of the players as they come into town. In picking Al Geiberger, for example, I didn't know that he was in a negative frame of mind about his putting. He had putted poorly the week before at Sutton and, I learned later, came to Congressional in a down mood. Yet his record all year was excellent and he seemed a good choice.

For now, I think I shall continue sticking out my chin. I am told that readers of the sports section enjoy the forecasts; I get a hint of this in the strong mail that comes in, suggesting that however hard it is to pick a winner, the copy is enjoyable to read. That's fine, but I hope that forecasting is something that all readers will begin doing for themselves. The point of predictions is not that one is proven right or wrong, but that regardless of the outcome, you watch or read about the tournament with intense interest. After all, why should I have all the pleasure?

The Winged Foot 500

"How a cart creaks," wrote Ivan Turgenev in *A Sportsman's Sketches.* Were the old Russian writer strolling at dawn or dusk today in one of the meadows we call golf courses, he would most likely make the same remark—not about a horse cart of peasants in from the steppes, but about a golf cart of hackers out for a romp.

For the person wishing to experience golf, rather than occasionally swing a club at a ball, the golf cart is no more an option for fairway mobility than Turgenev's horse cart. The golf course would be far more pleasant were it to remain a place where we can get around on our own, with no help from technology. Those who frown on the golf cart know that the menacing little vehicle offers few benefits to the golfer and fewer still to the course and the pleasures of the game. A case can be made that the cart is a threat to all three.

Those in good health who ride rather than walk are missing out on exercise that they most likely need and would enjoy. Countless doctors have advised their patients, "Take up golf. It will exercise your heart and get some fresh air into your lungs." The prescription has often been accepted as a painless, even pleasant, escape from routine once or twice a week. A year or so later, when the golfer returns for a checkup, the heart beat is low, firm and steady. The body is trim and blowing up the pulmonary function-test balloon is even possible.

Yet, many who take up the game for their health ride around the course in golf carts, believing that since walking makes them tired, walking should be avoided. Never mind that a basic stricture of health care is that exertion strengthens the heart muscles, just as surely as a lack of exercise weakens them.

It can't be known how many coronaries have been assisted by the golf cart since its introduction in the mid-1950s to those eager to tool along in the open-air easy-go wagon. But we are learning something about golf carts and broken bones. *Trial Magazine,* the journal read by lawyers specializing in litigation, ran an article in 1971 titled "The Unsafe Golf Cart." The author, Stanley Sacks, a Norfolk, Virginia, attorney, acknowledged that the vehicle was increasingly figuring in personal injury litigation. Doing research for a case involving a golfer permanently injured when thrown from his cart following a brake failure, Sacks investigated a number of patents on record at the U.S. Patent Office. He found that "in every instance, although the inventor enumerated the main object and other demonstrated characteristics of his particular golf cart, none listed a single safety feature among the reasons for his patent. While the inventors diligently sought after power, flexibility, maneuverability, lightness, compactness [and] long battery life . . . for the vehicle itself, none seemed concerned with the long life, safe use of even [temporary] security of the operator of the cart, its passengers, or those likely to be in the vicinity."

I know something about being "in the vicinity." Two summers ago, while playing on a hilly course in Washington, I was concentrating on an approach shot to the green. From above a slope to the left, I heard a noise that sounded like an animal scurrying through the underbrush. While I tried to ignore the distraction, the sound grew louder and closer. I looked up. A riderless cart wheel was coming toward me, wildly careening. Behind the wheel, the cart from which it had come loose was flip-flopping over the slope, on course to the pond below. I dove out of the wheel's way. Moments later two young men strolled over the hill. New members at this particular club, they were still laughing about their "crazy cart" and how it had taken off from under them. Their concern at the moment was not in wondering what became of the cart, or the people who might have been in its path, but in finding a phone booth where they could call the pro shop and summon another cart—to play the last two holes.

Not surprisingly, many clubs employ their own mechanics to repair the machines. I have gone out of my way to seek out these mechanics, and invariably they tell me that golf carts are put together even more flimsily than the American automobile, which I struggle to believe. At one course on Long Island, a cart mechanic explained, "I can work as hard as I want on any given cart, and I know that no matter what I do to it, the thing will be back in my garage in two or three months. The brakes are always wearing thin—not because the golfers ride them but because the metal is cheap and the cart's too heavy to be stopped by them. The wheels are continually out of line. I had a cart once that had to get a wheel alignment job after every round."

Family Safety magazine has acknowledged what that mechanic well knew—that many golf cart accidents "are apparently the result of poor construction." An article in that magazine in 1972 related the story of a Pittsburgh woman hospitalized for 11 weeks following a crash in which the steering wheel of the golf cart she had rented broke off and she was sent flying. In another case, recounted in the same article, two North Carolina golfers were bounding along in a golf cart when a wheel flew off. They were approaching a bridge at the time and the cart scored an extraordinary hole-in-one by plunging 15 feet into the pond below.

I have yet to meet a greenskeeper who spoke well of the golf cart. When the ground is wet, the wheels dig ruts into the turf. When the fairways are dry, the wheels tamp down the grass. Some courses restrict the vehicles to the rough, as though chewing up the taller grass is somehow less offensive; and many courses construct cartways, thus extending still further the reach of the pavement lobby. In all cases, though, the burden of repairing the damage falls to the greenskeeper and his staff, who already have trouble enough keeping the course green and fit on what are usually low budgets. "What can I do?" a greenskeeper at a Connecticut course said to me last year. "I talk about the problem to the chairman of the greens committee, to the pro, to the club president. But they just tell me to put up more direction signs around the course, so that the cart drivers won't run the damn things onto the greens."

If the greenskeeper's budget is low, the cart concessioner's is not. In some cases, the owner of the fleet is the club itself, other times the pro. Either way, the income is high. The original cost of a cart—$1,400 to $2,500—usually can be made up in a single season at rental rates from $6 to $10 per round. Some clubs are so eager for this profit that carts are mandatory: you can't walk even if you show a note from your doctor saying that your life depends on exercise. Clubs that are eager to leave the driving to you are also partly responsible for making caddies an endangered species. How can youngsters, or the adults, who show up in the caddy yards, make a loop if the bags are strapped to the cart?

If the golf cart ought to be avoided, it does serve at least one worthy purpose: Transporting those who are truly in poor health and wouldn't otherwise be able to get around. But for everyone else, it is a hazardous temptation. Too many other temptations in golf (hoping your opponent knee-putts, the boast and the occasional wager) are more appealing.

Your Bettor Self

Golf is for bettors, not gamblers. The difference, at least in my mind, is that bettors wager on themselves, with the ideas in mind that they have some control over the outcome and can grow as a result of the experience. Gamblers —at the race track or in the office football pool—have no control over the outcome of the action. Just as I can't recall ever gambling in my life, I can't recall ever playing 18 holes and not betting. I have ranged from $300 Nassaus with Bobby Riggs to 10 cent high-and-lows with Billy Graham. The betting has involved money, but only on a lower level. Above it are planes of competition with the self, where what you win or lose in dollars means nothing because either you have extended yourself to new areas of skill and feeling or you haven't. And you know within, either way.

I have played rounds in which I cleaned up, walking off the last green winning three ways in a Nassau and all the press bets both individually and team—yet feeling depressed about my play. I have had days when the opposite has happened—I've lost money but felt exhilarated.

One of these days was in the company of Bobby Riggs, and it is worth recounting. In recent years, Riggs has been known as a tennis hustler—playing challenge matches against Margaret Court and Billie Jean King, and roaming around the country mongering bets. When I came upon Riggs—in the summer months of 1959, when college was out—he was doing little else besides playing golf and I was doing little else besides earning my tuition by taking on all comers. My system was profitable until Riggs became one of the comers. He belonged to Plandome Country Club in Manhasset, Long Island. Riggs's problem at the club was that he could get no action from his sober clubmates. He was shunned as a brazen hustler who loved schemes to outsmart you, not outplay you.

I met Riggs when he showed up evenings at the North Shore Country Club, not far from Plandome, where I worked as the night-shift fairway waterman. Riggs would come out to hustle the pro shop workers, greenskeepers and local cops who had "privileges" in the evenings (in exchange for giving "speeding privileges" to members on the roads to and from the club). These were ragtag groups —working stiffs rushing around the course to beat sundown. Riggs, wearing the whites, erupting with talk, scampering about and his sheepdog hair flopping over his eyes added class, if that can be imagined.

I joined the matches. Riggs was an engaging kind of mole, ever burrowing up through layers of banter into a drive of intentness to beat you. He would play, he liked to boast, "anyone anytime anyplace for anything." But he wanted strokes if he thought you were better than he. His handicap was seven, an honest one I thought because he was in the 77 to 82 range. I was playing at scratch. After a few matches of assessing the other's game, we began playing regularly.

Out of that whole summer, the day I best remember was when Riggs took me for several hundred dollars. I forget the exact amount, but I recall vividly that my scores were 69, 67 and 33 for 45 holes over the hilly Plandome course. As if that weren't enough, both of us had earlier played 18 holes at nearby Wheatley Hills, in the qualifying round of the Long Island Amateur. I shot a 71, one under par, a score that was to win the medal by two strokes. Riggs, playing behind me, hacked to an 84. With both of us finishing around 11 A.M., Riggs suggested we "go play for real" now that the tournament was behind us (and he was out of it). We went to Plandome.

We played a $100 Nassau, ($100 for each—the front nine, back nine and overall 18) with Riggs getting seven shots. My three under par 69 helped me break even, because Riggs had a 76. But I remember not caring about the money, only the keenness of the play. Riggs was playing well, sinking a 20-footer after I had just holed one from 30 feet, or coming out of the woods for a hard par after I had relaxed and missed an easy birdie. But the pleasures of the competition were among the most satisfying I have ever had on the golf course. Riggs was what was called in the caddy yard "a betting fool," but wagering against him made me play some of the most remarkable golf shots I have ever hit.

After my 69, we went another 18—at about 4 P.M. We moved around the course fast. I shot 67 to his 73, and he won two ways: $200. It was vintage Riggs: exercising the skilled hustle, winning by enough but not so much as to discourage the victim. After 36 holes, he called out, "Let's go nine more. It's only 7:30." Riggs loved the word "only." It was "only" 230 yards over the water hazard, $10 says you can't make it." You were "only" two down, why not take a press bet? He was "only" a worn-out tennis bum, why not give him an extra stroke a side?

We played the last nine holes, but by now Riggs was unbeatable. He had a 36 to my 33 and, with his strokes, he won another hundred or two, I forget which. But I haven't forgotten the pleasures of that day: putting myself to a test of skill (against the course), of wits (against a superbly combative opponent) and of stamina (against myself).

When we go to the first tee and arrange a bet, it's best if all three challenges are involved. Winning or losing the money shouldn't matter. I have seen players come to life when they get involved in a bet; they are raised to new levels of pleasure. Not long ago, I was in a foursome in which I and three others had a $2 Nassau. The fourth player, not one of our regulars, was a strict Presbyterian for whom anything more than a 10 cent bet—really!— would predestine a man to damnation, and perhaps bank-ruptcy. On the first tee, while we made the $2 bet, I could see this fellow's stomach tightening, while the apple in his neck bobbed into the Big Choke position. The man wasn't cheap, he was nervous. In fact, he had plenty of money; he owned a Cadillac and was living on an income derived from real estate holdings. But the thought of losing $6 was strangling him so tightly that it might have been $600,000.

I took him for a partner. Or, factually, he was dumped on me by the other two who came together like a pair of pigeon hunters about to feast on the slowest bird in the flock. My partner was a 14-handicapper. He started out with three sevens. Then his bad play began: two nines and an eight. I kept taking press bets whenever we lost another two holes, but I couldn't carry the match. All my trembling partner asked as we left each green another hole down was, "How much do you think they'll take us for?" I'd answer, "No telling, just play hard." And then his Adam's apple would bob.

On the back nine, this hopeless case was suddenly trans-formed into a new self. He mixed six pars with three bogies. We won $16 on the back nine alone, a net gain of $6 from the $10 we lost on the front. What had happened to my partner? An old story: he had so disgraced himself on the front nine worrying about his lost bets, not to mention his wretched golf, that he was now purged of all self-humiliation. He could sink no deeper. He no longer cared now that we had discovered what a pathetic player he was. Freed, he played confident and skilled golf. It helped that I was patient with him and did not add to his anger by showing any dismay over his play.

A few months after this match, I saw him in the parking lot—in a new Cadillac, befitting the new man he had become—and he said he was now betting as much as a 20 cent Nassau. That was a 100 percent increase!—so I hailed it as a breakthrough and enjoyed good feelings about the part I had played in unloosening this Calvinist. He could have gone all his life like that.

One 10-center with whom I had little success was Billy Graham. I met him in Vero Beach, Florida, where he takes regular breaks from the strains of evangelism. Reverend Billy is a fine servant of the Lord but he can be hell to play with. He concedes all putts inside four feet, and sometimes longer. I believe he is dictated only by Christian charity: it is more blessed to give a four foot putt than to receive a four foot putt. The Kingdom of Heaven may be stormed that way, but on the greens you keep thinking of how mean-minded you are when you don't reciprocate by conceding ever longer and longer putts to Billy. He gives you a two-footer on No. 1, and you must return the favor by giving him a 2 1/2-footer on No. 2. On No. 3, he gives you a three-footer, and so on. It's all amiable and nothing but pure Christian spirit, but by the time you get to the back nine you are filled with guilt if Billy is forced to putt anything under four or five feet. In my game with him, we came to the 18th and he and his partner were one down. He had a 20-footer for a birdie to even the match. He rolled it by six feet. I had a seven-footer for a five. "Oh, that's good," called out Billy. "You've been dropping those all day." I had forgotten that I was, but what could I do but say that Billy's six-footer was good? He, too, had been making them all day, though again I would have had trouble saying on what holes, had I been asked. Both of us should have putted out these testers. I'm sure he would have blown his (he putts cross-handed after-all). But that was the devil in me, and Billy exorcised it. So our bet washed out because he won the last hole with a four to my five.

Betting, as I remind myself at times like that, means little in itself, unless it leads to self-challenge. With its stimulus we lift ourselves a little higher. All pleasures in life are based on stimuli that elevate us whether it be the pleasures of the spirit that the Trappists enjoy through their lives of contemplation and solitude, or the pleasures of the senses, as in enjoying good food or sex. We raise ourselves higher in momentary transcendence.

I notice this in even my most private form of betting, when I go out in the late evening for a few holes of solitary golf. I play four balls. I pit two Maxflis against two Titleists. Lowest total strokes wins the hole. Whichever ball "wins" the most evenings during a summer of play is the brand I give to friends as Christmas presents. But the real present is to myself: the little competition I create between Maxflis and Titleists gives me an opportunity to feel the intensity of play a little more. Something is "riding" on each shot.

In the end, that is the kind of betting I enjoy most when playing with others: an 18 hole match that involves each shot. Separate bets are made for the most drives in the fairway, closest to the pin on the par threes and on the approach shots to par fours and fives, fewest putts, fewest times in bunkers, most birdies, most pars and fewest bogies. Everything is covered, short of how many tees you break. With this many bets, you have a good chance of transcending because you can always begin a comeback. In too many methods of betting—the standard Nassau, for example—once you play badly you are out of it until the next nine begins or you take a press bet. But with something riding on each hole and each shot, you can revive yourself immediately. Isn't it true that a try at transcendence may be the reason that we go out to the golf course in the first place?

The Pros of Golf Prose

My own golf library has shelf space for every book I can find about the game. But the golf books for which I have special affection were written by three authors, each of them aware that the pleasures of reading about the game can be as deep as actually playing it. I have in mind Bobby Jones, P. G. Wodehouse and Bernard Darwin. I have been reading and rereading these three since I graduated from college, and I would have read them there had I been able to persuade the English department to put Jones, Wodehouse and Darwin on the required reading list.

Jones belonged on it. His own degree was in English literature from Harvard and his clear writing and quiet wit reveal the instincts of a natural writer. During his playing years, he was a keeper of notebooks and diaries, and from 1927 to 1935 he wrote a newspaper column twice weekly for the Bell Syndicate. One has only to read the copy produced by some of today's professionals to appreciate Jones. Besides his column, he wrote for magazines and for the scripts of his own instructional films. Jones estimated that over the years he wrote at least half a million words on golf. Today, many of these polished words can be found in three Jones's books: *Down the Fairway* (Minton, Balch and Company, 1927), *Golf Is My Game* (Doubleday, 1966) and *Bobby Jones On Golf* (Doubleday, 1966). The last is my personal preference because in it we get both the youthful and the mature Jones, since the book has many of the pieces he wrote in the '20s and '30s but expanded on in the '60s.

The parts of *Bobby Jones On Golf* which suggest that here was a special man occur when Jones thinks aloud: "I remember reading in an English newspaper after I had won the British Open at St. Andrews, an editorial that made a point of the slight margin of superiority shown by the winner of a tournament over the rest of the field. In this particular championship, I had won by the greatest margin I had ever had, yet as the editorial pointed out, my advantage of six strokes, however big it may have looked, when reduced to percentage, read only 2.105 percent, or 1 1/2 strokes in each round in which an average of a little less than seventy-two strokes were used. I suppose it is consideration of a slender margin such as this that led J. H. Taylor to say that the difference between the winner and near-winner is the ability on the part of the successful contestant to be ever on the lookout against himself."

Jones's writing flows with gentle dissents, though it is clear that he is in the tradition of the Scots who temperamentally had low tolerance for guff and bunk. He is ever alert to stray thinking that, like the stray golf shot, easily goes off course. "I have not regarded seriously the tendency of some people to endow golfers with superhuman powers. Because on occasion a few players have staged spectacular finishes to retrieve victory by last-minute rallies, I have heard it said of them that they are able to pull off whatever is necessary to win. Such an idea is absurd, for if these men were capable of playing golf as they willed, they would never place themselves so that they had to beat par to win." Jones may have had in mind the 12 foot clutch putt he made on the last green in the 1929 U.S. Open at Winged Foot. He sunk it to tie Al Espinosa, but Jones's "miracle finish" was necessitated by a triple bogey at the 8th and another at the 15th.

As a competitor who won 13 titles before retiring at 28—or, putting it as the golf writer Charles Price did, "winning 62 percent of the national championships he entered"—Jones is at his most perceptive when recounting some of the things that run through a player's mind as the pressure rises. "It is difficult for a person who has not been mixed up in these things to understand what it means to play a competitive round against opponents who cannot be seen. In an Open Championship, one's imagination runs riot. A burst of applause or a cheer from a distant part of the course is always interpreted as a blow from some close pursuer, when it may mean no more than that some obscure competitor has holed a chip shot while another player's waiting gallery happened to be watching. It may not mean a thing, and even if it does, it can't be helped. But it is difficult to view it that way. One always feels that he is running from something without knowing exactly what nor where it is."

As a man whose intellect and spirit fed on a different diet than most golfers, Jones sustained a balance about the game. He insisted that his life should have a wholeness to it, with golf a part of it but assuredly not the only part. When he decided at the end of the season in 1930 to "withdraw entirely from golfing competition," one reason was his desire "to avoid getting myself into such a position that

I would have to keep on playing." He wanted to use his law degree, and had little desire for his father—"not a rich man"—to keep paying his way as he chased from one tournament to another. How refreshing it is to reflect on Jones's decisiveness in getting out, especially now when so many athletes hang on long after their glory days. Jones said in 1930: "Fourteen years of intensive tournament play in this country and abroad had given me about all I wanted in the way of hard work in the game. I had reached a point where I felt that my profession required more of my time and effort, leaving golf in its proper place, a means of obtaining recreation and enjoyment."

Perhaps because of his age—28—or perhaps because the flow of his competitive juices could not be dried up as casually as he thought, Jones the contemplative later had second thoughts about his early retirement. "There is a school of Oriental philosophy, I am told, which holds that the aim of life should be the perfection of personality or character, and that sufferings, joys, and achievements mean nothing except as they influence the development of this personality or character. I hope the analogy will not appear too ridiculous, but it has been thinking along such a line that has uncovered the only real regret I have ever had about quitting competitive golf when I was only twenty-eight years of age."

That comment is from *Golf Is My Game*. As a mix of instruction and memoir, the book contains some of the most touching lines ever written in golf literature. Jones tells of his last visit to St. Andrews, in 1958, when the Town Clerk of that Scottish village "accorded Mr. Jones the privileges of a Burgess and Guild Brother of the city of St. Andrews." The last American to be asked in for that honor was Benjamin Franklin of Philadelphia, in 1759.

In the last chapter of the book, tenderly called "St. Andrews—A Short Love Story," Jones recalls some of his remarks to the townspeople on the day of his being honored.

He spoke of earlier days, when he was in full health and not suffering from a crippling muscular disease that was slowing him down at only age 56. "My thoughts are not of championships and trophies as I stand here tonight. You people possess a sensitivity which causes you to be able to extend cordiality and express friendliness in the most ingenious way . . . I could take out of my life everything except my experiences at St. Andrews and I'd still have a rich, full life."

The two 1966 Jones books are still in most libraries, but I have never had much luck in locating copies of his 1927 autobiography, *Down the Fairway* (written with O. B. Keeler). The Library of Congress has a copy. The others, presumably, are either in home libraries or waiting to be discovered by browsers in dusty secondhand bookstores or at such events as the famous Vassar Book Sale in Washington. That is where I found my copy—for 25 cents! In the autobiography, published when Jones was 25 no less, there are hints of the inner man who wanted more out of life than just the pleasures of golf. He tells of his handling the "subjective nerve-tension" of tournament golf. "Years ago I discovered that the best preparation for a big tournament, for me, was as much rest as I could acquire, in the twenty-four hours before the opening gun. In my younger days I liked to play a lot of golf, right up to the day competition began. Often I'd play 36 holes the day before it started. Now I try always to schedule the little preliminary practice season, of three or four days, so that the last day I can rest. In bed, often, with a book. I remember the day before the national amateur championship at Flossmoor. I stopped in bed and read Papini's *Life of Christ,* a book with an odd fascination to me."

This youthful interest in religion apparently stayed with Jones during his adult years. In fact, in his dying days, in the winter of 1971, after years of uncomplaining acceptance of the disease that had tortured and crippled his body, Jones was received into the Roman Catholic Church.

As for the public's last memories of Jones, we have his appearances at the Masters every spring, when, in his wheelchair, he was as avid a spectator as he had been a player. The pleasures of watching were felt as deeply by this man of immeasurable feelings as the youthly pleasures of playing.

While Jones wrote about his own sensitivity to golf, as well as his detachment from the sport, the joys and merriment of the game have had no finer chronicler than P. G. Wodehouse. At his death, at 93, in early 1975, he was known worldwide as an incomparable specialist in fantasy. For members of that secret society who tire quickly of being rational and adult, and who wish that search parties for Hidden Truths would stop occasionally to rest their feet, a Wodehouse story on golf is a delight. The moods created by Wodehouse—merry, spirited and light—offer a welcome release. Wodehouse's fiction describes the dotty highborn and their devotions to playfulness.

In March, 1974, Simon & Schuster did the sensible thing and put out *The Golf Omnibus,* a book that contains the 31 golf stories Wodehouse wrote over five decades. Golf has no storyteller like him. The Wodehouse characters who play on his fictional fairways have long been on the endangered species list, clubmen of impeccable snobbery for whom life's severest agony is a caddy who has hiccups, or an unraked bunker or a slice of seed-cake that a butler —not jumping to the bell—is too slow in bringing to the veranda. A Wodehouse golfer dresses in serge or flannel knickerbockers, has inherited his fortune rather than dirtily worked for it and knows that swank is what the old money has, while chic is what the new money must settle for.

The brightest luminary in the Wodehouse clubhouse is The Oldest Member. It is he who tells the stories. The Oldest Member is white-haired, wise and mannered. All clubs used to have sages like him until the clubs began allowing in (as the Edwardians in Wodehouse fiction would say) the rabble and muck, in their Torinos and alligator shirts, and playing Woolworth golf balls. The Oldest Member always sits in his favorite chair on the Wodehouse club terrace and spins tales to those youngsters between 10 and 80 who wander by. "To the philosophical student of golf like myself," the Oldest Member says, "perhaps the most outstanding virtue of this noble pursuit is the fact that golf is a medicine for the soul. Its great service to humanity is that it teaches human beings that, whatever petty triumphs they may have achieved in other walks of life, they are after all merely human. It acts as a corrective against sinful pride. I attribute the insane arrogance of the later Roman emperors almost entirely to the fact that, never having played golf, they never knew that strange chastening humility which is engendered by a topped chip-shot. If Cleopatra had been ousted in the first round of the Ladies' Singles, we should have heard a lot less of her proud imperiousness."

In his chair and in his sagacity, The Oldest Member offers counsel to the junior members. Often he tries to console a young golfer of skill whose belle is being won by a rival. "Cheer up," says the Oldest Member to one such unfortunate. "I know just how you feel, but rest assured that all will be well. Josh Hook's string tricks may be sweeping the girl off her feet for the moment but his glamour will pass. She will wake tomorrow morning her true self again, thankful that she has the love of a good man who seldom shoots worse than eighty-three."

The Oldest Member, who believes that marriages arranged on the 19th hole prove to be stable, says, "It is an excellent thing that women should be encouraged to take up golf. There are, I admit, certain drawbacks attendant on their presence on the links. I shall not readily forget the occasion on which a low, raking drive of mine at the 11th struck the ladies' tee box squarely and came back and stunned my caddie, causing me to lose stroke and distance. Nevertheless, I hold that the advantages outnumber the drawbacks. Golf humanizes women, humbles their haughty natures, tends, in short, to knock out of their systems a certain modicum of the superciliousness, that swank, which makes wooing a tough proposition for the diffident male."

That wisdom from the veranda is as delightful today as ever. The ingenuity of a Wodehouse story lies not only in the plot—which thickens, then coagulates into confusion and turns viscid with twists—but also in the absence of anger or meanness in any of the characters. Nowhere among the stories about Bertie Wooster, Freddie Threepwood, Jeeves or the Oldest Member does a calorie burn for anything except the pursuit of a sunny life. Occasionally someone gets impatient or flustered—"I've never heard of anything as ridiculous in my life," she ejaculated. "Do you mean to say that he is waiting till he is good at golf before he asks me to marry him?"—but as Wodehouse wrote in his autobiography, his creatures are always "genial and good-tempered." How many of our modern novelists could go a paragraph, not to mention 60,000 words, about the contented? "In these days," Wodehouse wrote in 1961, "when everybody hates the insides of everybody else, anyone who is not snarling at something—or at everything—is an anachronism."

Unlike many humorists who secretly believe their tales portend of high philosophy or deep metaphysics, Wodehouse seldom got beyond himself. "The trouble about reaching the age of 92," he wrote in the preface to *The Golf Omnibus,* one of his last books, "is that regrets for a misspent life are bound to creep in, and whenever you see me with a furrowed brow you can be sure that what is on my mind is the thought that if only I had taken up golf earlier and devoted my time to it instead of fooling about writing stories and things, I might have got my handicap down to under 18. If only they put a putter in my hands when I was four and taught me the use of the various clubs, who knows what heights I might not have reached. It is this reflection that has always made my writing so sombre, its whole aroma like that of muddy shoes in a Russian locker room."

As for his own place in the game, Wodehouse wrote, "I was never much of a golfer. Except for that glorious day at Aiken [when he won a striped umbrella in a hotel tournament], I was always one of the dregs, the sort of man whose tee shots, designed to go due north, invariably went nor-nor-east or in a westerly direction. But how I loved the game."

Contrasted against our good fortune in having all of Wodehouse in one volume is the inaccessibility of Bernard Darwin. Whenever a friend is going to England, I give him a few dollars and ask that he scout around the bookstores for some of the Bernard Darwin titles I don't have. As the golf writer for *The London Times* from 1907 to 1953, much of Darwin's journalism—reportage and essays—was so finely written that it was regularly collected into books. But they are hard to find in this country.

One of the Darwin masterpieces that a friend brought back from London was *British Golf,* a slim book that tells about the history of the game in Britain. In the preface, Darwin writes: "Golf differs from almost every other game in that every piece of land on which it is played has its own characteristics and scenery and flavour. It is no flat, bare expanse, but is made up of miniature hills and valleys, each with a personality of its own. A longer book than this could easily be filled with the joys and beauties of British courses, but then a much longer book still would not suffice for the deeds of the famous golfers who have played over them. Rather than fall between the two stools I have to make my choice, and I choose the golfers. The play is the thing; the human interest comes before the geographical, and with that apology I shall plunge straight ahead."

His plunging came naturally, because Darwin had the education of a scholar—a Cambridge degree (from Trinity College), plus studies in the law—and he was the grandson of Charles Darwin, the evolutionist. He was a lifelong student of Charles Dickens, produced two books on him, and wrote children's stories as well. As an amateur golfer, Darwin's high moment came at age 45 when he was a semifinalist in the 1921 British Amateur, an achievement that earned him a place next year on the Walker Cup team. He won his singles match (played over the National Golf Links, Southampton, Long Island) against his American opponent, after being called in to play when the team captain fell ill.

With that in his background, Darwin ranged far in his coverage of golf for the *Times.* The paper did not believe in by-lines—Darwin articles were labelled "By Our Golf Correspondent"—but readers knew the author by the style. He brought as much wit and elegance to his stories about yesterday's play as he did when sitting back to reflect on the game's history. He enjoyed discussing golf's origins as a way of leading up to what he always saw as the game's glorious present. He wrote in 1923 of the low social rank that professionals once endured, and went on from there to discuss the amateurs. "The state of things, has, it is needless to say, long since been changed and the professional has been for years the respected and self-respecting member of society that we know today. The amateur has changed too in that he has now as a rule to work for his living and cannot give so much time to the game as he once could. That anonymous amateur of the aphorism could presumably play golf to his heart's content, could play it at least as often as any professional. If we scan the list of the amateurs who first became famous figures in the game we find for the most part that they were so fortunately situated as to have a great deal of leisure. They might have some business or profession but it was seldom of a very exacting character. They might have other interests and amusements besides golf, witness young Tommy Morris's bitter cry to Mr. Gilbert Mitchell Innes: 'I cannot understand Mr. Innes, when he's playing as fine a game as ony mortal man ever played, leaving gowf to rin after a wheen stinking beasts, and then comin' back, no able to hit a ba.' The distinguished amateur might be guilty of such a lamentable desertion of the links but it was his deliberate act; he could generally play as much golf as he wanted. Those so happily circumstanced have grown fewer as time has gone on and it is not hard to prophesy that, in golf as in first-class cricket, they will in the post-war world grow fewer still."

When I go to golf tournaments and visit the press tents, I make it a practice of talking with the golf writers about Darwin. Shockingly, I come upon more and more of them who say, "Who's he—never heard of the guy." Sometimes I try to tell them, other times I leave them be, but always I am astonished that their editors would actually assign them to cover golf without first having suggested they read Darwin. That raises the question of whether or not the editors themselves are knowledgeable about Darwin, a question that leaves me sweating in fear of possible negative answers.

It was a delight a few years ago to review for my newspaper the wonderful book, *No Cheering in the Press Box* (edited by Jerome Holtzman, Holt, Rinehart and Winston, 1973), and find the words of Al Laney on Darwin. Laney, whose prose graced the old *New York Herald Tribune* for years, called the British master "the best sportswriter of all . . . He was an extraordinary reporter. Darwin had a great influence on my writing, so much so that I was afraid for a time I was trying to imitate him. Even to this day it embarrasses me when someone says, 'I like your stuff, it reminds me of Darwin.' "

Laney knew Darwin, or at least was at some of the tournaments with him. Shortly before the British Open in 1926, at Lytham St. Annes, a friend—Bob Harlow, Walter Hagen's manager—offered to introduce Laney to Darwin. "I stood in such awe of Darwin that I said, 'No, don't introduce me. I don't want to meet him.'

"Harlow insisted. He said, 'C'mon, he won't bite.' He took me over and presented me. But Darwin did bite. I stuck out my hand to shake with him, and he didn't take my hand. Instead, he started to talk to Archie Compston, a famous golf pro at the time. I was crushed. Oh, gee, I turned away, crying."

The next day, Harlow berated Darwin for his behavior. Laney continues: "The next week at the British Open at Lytham, Darwin hooked his arm in mine at the first tee and walked me down the fairway. He showed himself very friendly, just talking in generalizations. I knew I was in the presence of a master. I was kind of bewildered. Lytham opens with a par three, so it wasn't much of a walk, and he dismissed me gently. At any rate it was obvious he had done what he intended to do, sort of make amends. From then on until the war I saw Darwin at every tournament I covered. He was always civil enough. But he didn't communicate. No one was ever close to Darwin." Laney's assessment of the *Times* man is succinct: "Darwin was an essayist, and we don't have that anymore. We have columnists. The columnist tells us how we should think. The essayist tells us what he thinks."

To read Darwin is to receive from journalism exactly what it can provide at its most illuminating moments: transportation to the scene. Filing from the Old Course at St. Andrews, when Bobby Jones won the 1921 British Open, Darwin wrote: "Many vivid pictures remain in my mind's eye from this day, but there is one in particular. Bobby lay just short of the home green in the hollow called The Valley of Sin. He ran his long putt up dead, and the crowd stormed up the slope and waited breathless for a moment at the crest. He popped his ball in, and the next instant there was to be seen no green and no Bobby—nothing but a black and seething mass from which there ultimately emerged the victor bourne on enthusiastic shoulders and holding his famous putter, Calamity Jane, over his head in a frantic effort to preserve it."

Darwin died in 1961 at age 85. Although his autobiography, *The World That Fred Made,* tells us much about his thoughts and feelings, we are lucky to have *Mostly Golf,* a biography by Peter Ryde, Darwin's successor at the *Times.* It is a new book, published in England in the autumn of 1976. My copy is on the way at this writing, and I have set aside shelf space for it.

The golf world that Jones, Wodehouse and Darwin wrote about is gone, but the excellence and vibrancy of their writing not only remains, it grows. When I go to golf courses that I know will be crowded, I put in my golf bag a book of Jones, Wodehouse or Darwin. On the course, while waiting 15 or 20 minutes on the tee, or standing in the fairway waiting for a clear green, I reach into the bag. A paragraph or two of, say, Jones is like a conversation with an old friend, one who knows something about the game and is sure to say it well. I suspect that I may present an odd sight—a bookman on the fairways—but if I am there on the course to be uplifted by the game itself, why not be uplifted also by communion with golf's finest writers?